# SIDEWAYS ATLANTA

## A Field Guide to Offbeat Attractions in the "City Too Busy to Hate"

by
**Suzanne Winterberger**
and
**Bill Tomey**

Published by
the Creative Intelligence Agency
Edinboro, Pennsylvania

# SIDEWAYS ATLANTA:
## A field guide to the offbeat attractions in the "City Too Busy to Hate"
### by
## Suzanne Winterberger & Bill Tomey

Published by:
Creative Intelligence Agency
P.O. Box 77
Edinboro, PA 16412 U.S.A.

Manufactured in the United States of America

This limited edition of *Sideways Atlanta* is one of 500 copies produced in November, 1995.

**ISBN: 0-9650333-5-X**

# Table of Contents

# Dedication to Sideways

This book is dedicated to Sideways, a dog.

Thrown out of a car at the Varsity Restaurant in 1945, her injuries caused her to walk sideways. Adopted by the Georgia Tech community at large, Sideways attended classes, slept in the dorms, and ate at the Dining Hall. She was kidnapped by the University of Georgia (Athens) and rescued. Students bailed her out everytime the dog-catchers nabbed her. Sadly, Sideways died after eating rat poison. She is buried on the Georgia Tech campus.

# Acknowledgments

We would like to thank our many friends and family members, without whose advice, encouragement, and/or willingness to be dragged all over Atlanta, this book would never have happened:

Baby Sue, Louise Chambers, John Eisenmann, Michael Enns,
Larry Fertick, Patrick Flynn, Jon Guthrie,
Jon Hayano, David "Biscuit" Holliman,
our editor Colleen Holmes, Mark Krell,
Robert Sherer, Susie Smith,
Rick Thompson, "Hosta Tom" Tillery,
Sandra Thornton, Don Williams, Denis Wright,
and the many fine dogs we have been honored to know.

# Orientation

Atlanta has an amazing capacity to grow, change, transform, adapt, and learn from its history, making it today a beautiful city of spunk, wisdom, and diversity. It's a city of not just a little bit of hustle, a place where one can simultaneously live in a small town neighborhood and be plagued and/or entertained by big city life. It's been described as both a big small town and a little big city. Atlanta's history peels away like the layers of an onion. It has been Bill's and my great joy to peel back layer after layer to discover wonderful people, places, and stories. It has also been our great sorrow to find that many of these places no longer exist or exist only as a shadow of their former grandeur. The sites of some of our favorite stories have fallen prey to urban renewal and now get only a quick nod along the interstate. The tales lie buried underneath an interchange, a parking lot, or a stadium.

You see, Atlanta has this habit of rising up from the ashes of its own destruction and rebuilding itself completely. The city has had several growths. Nearly everyone knows about Sherman's March through Georgia, when the entire city was burned to the ground. Similarly, Atlanta suffered through two major riots in 1902 and 1906, both of which affected large areas of the city.

Downtown Atlanta was almost completely razed in the 1970s in the name of urban renewal. Many, many of the old buildings and historic sites we went looking for were long gone by the time we found the spot. Very few of the sites have been replaced by something appropriate to the history of Atlanta, and too seldom is something very interesting now standing.

We don't really mind loitering on a miscellaneous street-corner in the middle of urban development and saying, "well, this was the spot so & so did such & such." We do like knowing where things happened and we like bringing this information together. We hope you residents of Atlanta will find wonderful new things to see and do, and we hope visitors will take a little bit of extra time to see some of the places we've found, and that you'll come on back later to see more.

The book is divided up in several ways. Subject matter tours such as a Sports (Tomahawkin') or Segregation are for those persons who like to follow a theme when exploring a new place. We have geographic tours for those of you who suddenly find yourselves lost and on Ponce de Leon Avenue, for example. A history buff might first want to consult the chapters on the Brief History, the Peachtree Trail, or the War of Northern Aggression. Lovers of popular culture can turn to the sections on Ponce de Leon Avenue, the James Dean Date, or Little Five Points. American culture buffs will be especially interested in the Civil Rights Tour, Margaret Mitchell, and the Wren's Nest. True offbeats, however, will get special satisfaction out of visiting the Ku Klux Klan Supply Store, the Apparitions of the Blessed Virgin Mary, or a possible UFO landing site.

This field guide assumes you will be using a car. Due to the complex and often logically-incomprehensible layout of the city, we do recommend you have a good map with you at all times. We suggest a Gousha map . . . all of our directions in this field guide are based on the Gousha. All phone numbers, unless otherwise specified, are in the 404 area code.

Please note: in Atlanta there are many "Peachtree" labels (lanes, roads, plazas, etc.) but only one authentic, honest-to-goodness "Peachtree Street." Peachtree Street is a major artery which begins below downtown and ends out in the suburb of Doraville. We use Peachtree Street as one of our landmarks from which to begin some of the driving tours.

We would caution the visitor to use common sense while driving in unfamiliar areas of the city of Atlanta. It is never a bad idea to keep your doors locked and your windows up, and we would not recommend your wandering around aimlessly anywhere late at night. During the day, however, and on into the early evening, there is no reason to be paranoid, just alert.

This field guide will not be complete until it is used by you, the reader. In the back of this book is a request for your help in compiling future editions. If you find a special place you feel should be included, please let us know. Meanwhile, we hope your visits to Atlanta are thoroughly satisfying.

Happy exploring!

*The authors*

# SIDEWAYS ATLANTA

Standing Peachtree

Grave of Martin and Susan DeFoor in
the Montgomery Family Cemetery

# Chapter 1
# A Brief History of Atlanta
(with special thanks to Mr. Franklin Garrett,
our personal hero & Shining Light of Atlanta)

Most accounts of the story of Atlanta begin with the pounding of a railroad surveyor's stake into the ground in 1837. The stake was located close to the center of what is now downtown Atlanta, and served to initiate a rapid growth in railroads and industry.

The earliest known account of the region, however, dated 1782, is found in the annals of the Revolutionary War. The settlement was called **Standing Peachtree,** located in what is now Northwestern Atlanta, along the Chattahoochee River. Named for a nearby peach tree, it belonged to the Creek Indians, who won the region from the Cherokees in a series of ballgames. Five trails converged at the point where Peachtree Creek and the Chattahoochee River meet.

During the War of 1812, the Creeks allied with the British. Fort Peachtree was established at the Standing Peachtree settlement. The fort was used for a few years, then gradually abandoned. In 1837, Colonel James Montgomery built a ferry to cross the Chattahoochee. Standing Peachtree is located in the Atlanta Water Pumping Station at 2630 Ridgewood Road, NW (355-8299).

A replica of Fort Peachtree is located here at the Water Pumping Station, along with three historical markers. You can see the Chattahoochee River here, and walk down to the river itself. This is also a good kayak entry point.

Activity in what is now Atlanta "proper" began around 1822 when Richard Todd and his family bought land in the area which is now, roughly, Ponce de Leon Avenue and North Highland Avenue. Descendents of the original Todd family still live at 816 Greenwood Avenue. A graveyard in back of the house (not the original house) contains the remains of members of the original family.

> From the Atlanta History Center on West Paces Ferry Road, head west till the road forks (just past the Governor's mansion on the right). Take the left fork (Moore's Mill road) past Route 75. After you go down a hill and cross a creek with two inaccessible historical markers, look for Ridgewood road on your right. Go up about one mile; the entrance will be on your left. The gates are open M-F, 9-4.
>
> Continue west on Moore's Mill Road to the end. Check out the historical marker on your right at the corner of Moore's Mill and Bolton. Go straight (through the parking lot), and straight across Boulevard . . . head for the pharmacy. Just to the left of the store, hidden in the brush on top of a knoll, is the Montgomery family cemetery, resting place of some of Atlanta's first citizens.

Hardy Ivy is considered to be Atlanta's first permanent white settler. He married one of Richard Todd's daughters. Ivy bought land near downtown Atlanta in 1833, building his house at the corner of Ellis and Courtland Streets. Also known as College Hill, this was the site of the short-lived Atlanta Female College, which graduated only one class before the outbreak of the War Between the States.

It is not clear why Ivy gets credit for being Atlanta's first settler, permanent or otherwise, as Dr. Chapman Powell built **The Medicine House** earlier, in 1826, on the Shallowford Trail (at what is now Clairmont and N. Decatur). This was a place where Indians came for medical treatment. A convenience store now sits on the site; in 1961 the house itself was moved to Stone Mountain, and is used as a slave house in the plantation exhibit.

In 1835, the **White Hall Tavern** was opened by Charner Humphries in Southwest Atlanta. Located on the east side of Lee between Gordon and Park, the tavern, which did not survive the War Between the States, served as an important stop as a road junction and stagecoach route.

The official surveyor's stake marking Atlanta was driven on May 12, 1837, and the town was named **Terminus**. The first baby, Julia Carlisle, was born in 1842. In 1843, the town was renamed Marthasville, and in 1844, the official first baby (ie: white, male) was born. He was Billings Socrates Ivy, or "Sock," the son of Henry P. Ivy and grandson of Hardy Ivy. Finally, in 1845, legislation brought the city of Atlanta into being. The name was protested as being "strange and alien," but in reality, was named after the Western and Atlantic Railroad (feminine version). For many years, however, the name was misspelled and mispronounced as "Atalanta."

Atlanta was, and still is, a tough town. Several notorious dens of iniquity sprouted up right from its beginning. **"Murrel's Row,"** downtown at the corner of Decatur and Pryor was notorious for cock-fighting. A haven for outlaws, it was dedicated to the legend of Tennessee badguy John A. Murrel. Nearby was "Slabtown," at Decatur and Pratt. **"Snake Nation"** covered a large area centered around Peters and Fair. Well known for gambling, murders, and prostitution, it was also a safe haven for a large criminal population and now is an artists' warehouse area.

Other great strongholds of crime included areas named "Hobo Hollow," "Beaver Slide," "Tight Squeeze," "Buttermilk Bottom," and "Humbug Square." **Tight Squeeze** was located at the intersection of Peachtree Road and Tenth Street. On the eastern side of Peachtree was a ravine extending down toward Piedmont Avenue, where the disreputable community sprang up right after the War Between the States. It was said that it took a mighty tight squeeze to come through the place with one's life and health intact, hence the name, Tight Squeeze. Just north of Decatur, on the eastern side of Ivy, was located **Beaver Slide**, another haven for the rough element, until it was burned in an effort to stem an outbreak of smallpox in the late 1880s. **Humbug Square**, then a vacant lot bordered by Alabama, Whitehall, Loyd, and the railroad, now in Underground Atlanta, attracted traveling con men, medicine shows, and charlatans of all kinds.

The **first jail** was built in 1848 at Pryor and Alabama, mostly to house runaway slaves. Criminals remanded to this simple facility, however, were often immediately liberated by their cronies, who merely hoisted up the side of the building to allow their pals to squeeze out.

Near this same site, in 1850, Atlanta's **first fire** was set by robbers as a diversion to their robbery of the Georgia Railroad Freight Depot. By 1851, upright citizens of Atlanta, tired of crime and violence, founded the Moral Party to combat the forces of evil. The criminal element, not to be outdone, promptly founded the Rowdy Party, headquartered at Decatur and Ivy. Both parties nominated candidates for mayor. Although the Moral Party won, the Rowdy Party did not quiet down for quite some time.  Sand was shot from a cannon at the Mayor's front porch, and sporadic threats were made from Murrel's Row.  Eventually, however, moralists, nicknamed the "White Caps," raided Snake Nation.  The men were beaten and told to leave town; the women were taken to Decatur and dumped off.  When Snake Nation and Slabtown were destroyed by fire, momentum was lost and the criminal element dispersed.

A few other "firsts" remain noteworthy.  As with so many other firsts, they are always open to contradiction.  In 1847, the first Baptist Church was built at the northwest corner of Forsyth and Walton.  Baptisms were conducted at the nearby Walton Springs.  **Walton Springs** was also the site of the city's first amusement park, which boasted the world's first ferris wheel.  The wheel, operated by Antonio Maquino, was forty feet in diameter and needed "two husky Negroes" to crank it.  People sat in wooden crates.  It wasn't until forty years later that the ferris wheel officially made its debut in Paris and at the Chicago World's Fair.

Another interesting first was **the first burial in Oakland Cemetery** in 1850.  Dr. James Nissen, a visitor to Atlanta, died and was buried in the new cemetery right after his jugular vein was cut, just to make sure he was really dead! Apparently, it was not highly unusual for a person to be buried alive (although how would anyone know?), and Nissen was especially fearful of meeting that particular fate.  The cutting ceremony was performed at the graveside.

A highly detailed and intensive study of the early history of Atlanta was made by Mr. Franklin M. Garrett.  Volumes I and II of *Atlanta and Environs*, originally published in 1954, consist of more than 2,000 pages of dense information covering the years up to 1930.  Mr. Garrett, who should be considered a National Living Treasure, received Atlanta's Shining Light Award in 1993 for his lifetime of work as the city's premier historian.  Visitors to the Atlanta History Center might be lucky enough to run into him; the center also hosts an occasional "Stump Franklin Garrett Night."  **The Atlanta History Center** should be your first stop before beginning your exploration of the city.  It is located at 130 West Paces Ferry Road, just west of Peachtree Road in Buckhead.  Call 814-4000 for more information on their many interesting activities, tours, and programs.

# Chapter 2
# The Peachtree Trail
### (and other ancient roads)

**M**any of the roads and trails in old Atlanta exist today only underneath current routes through the city. Atlanta's first trail, the Peachtree Trail, stretched thirty miles between Fort Peachtree and Fort Daniel at Hog Mountain, in what is now Gwinnett County.

Peachtree Trail is a good driving tour, with several interesting sites along the way. You should begin at the origin of the trail, at **Standing Peachtree**. From Standing Peachtree, take Moore's Mill Road east to Paces Ferry, and head towards Buckhead. Along the way, you will pass the **Governor's Mansion** on West Paces Ferry (on the left). This drive takes you through some of the wealth and glamour that is the Buckhead section of Atlanta. **The Atlanta History Center** will be on your right as you approach the intersection of Paces Ferry with Routes 9, 19, and 141.

> **From the Atlanta History Center, head northeast up route 141. Also known as Peachtree Road, route 141 follows the old trail along what used to be known as Peachtree Ridge. In the town of Chamblee, Peachtree Road branches off to the right from route 141. Continue along until the road zig-zags into routes 13 and 23, also known as the Buford Highway. Eventually the road leads you to Suwanee, Flowery Branch, and Hog Mountain, but we did not find this to be particularly scenic.**

In order to head north on route 141, you must turn left

just after the Atlanta History Center, at Paces Ferry Place. Go to Irby, turn right, and at Roswell (routes 9 & 19), turn right. At the intersection of Irby and Roswell, you will see the **Cotton Exchange Building** (3155 Roswell). This building, now occupied by a law firm, is reputed to be a former Ku Klux Klan factory where robes were manufactured.

At the large intersection just south of the Cotton Exchange, turn left, back onto Paces Ferry, and make your first left. Turn right on Peachtree Road (route 141). If you are not interested in seeing the KKK robe factory, simply proceed on Paces Ferry straight through the main intersection, make your first left, then turn right onto route 141.

Peachtree Road passes the modern shopping havens Lenox Square and Phipps Plaza. You might want to make a stop at Oglethorpe University (on the left), home of the **Crypt of Civilization**, sealed May 25, 1940. It is due to be opened in 8113. Deeded to the U.S. government, it is located in the basement of the Hearst Building near the bookstore. It contains many interesting items, including a toilet brush, eyelash curlers, fish hooks, a golfball, Lincoln Logs, and the voice of Hitler! A more complete list is available at the University.

Soon after passing Oglethorpe, the trail branches off from route 141 onto New Peachtree Road in the town of **Chamblee**. Chamblee is antique heaven! Can you fit an entire 1940s soda fountain in your suitcase? Do you need your own gas pump in your front yard? Did you ever wonder where all those old service station signs and logos end up? Chamblee! If you are a pop culture enthusiast, plan to spend at least half a day here.

We have not found the route past Chamblee to be particularly scenic or interesting. However, if you have time to spare, it is a nice ride to continue north from Flowery Branch up and around Lake Lanier, heading northwest on route 60 at Gainesville to **Dahlonega**, the site of Georgia's gold rush. Dahlonega offers the visitor a gold mine museum, opportunities to pan for gold, and an interesting downtown shopping district. You can return to Atlanta via route 19, which eventually runs right back past the Paces Ferry Road intersection where you started heading north.

Another old trail is one that runs from the Ponce de Leon Springs (on Ponce de Leon Avenue, at the old Sears building) up to Flowery Branch. A tablet on the Sears building commemorates this trail, which runs, roughly, up Highland Avenue to Briarcliff (route 42), eventually connecting with route 23 (the Buford Highway), and on to Flowery Branch.

# Chapter 3
# Ponce de Leon

**P**once de Leon Avenue is one of the most interesting and colorful areas of the city. Running roughly east-west from midtown and the celebrated Fox Theatre, the road ends near Stone Mountain, site of three Confederate Generals racing across the rockface. By far the most interesting stretch of Ponce, however, lies between the Fox Theatre (at Peachtree) and the Plaza Theatre (at Highland).

**Yancey Spring** was the original Ponce de Leon landmark. Located near Ponce de Leon Place, where the railroad track crosses Ponce, Yancey Spring was buried in 1868 in order to build the railroad. New springs were found nearby, right on the future site of the gigantic Sears Building. Two springs were discovered, each with a different kind of water, but both springing separately out of the same rock. The springs were separated by only six inches of rock. When it was reported the waters cured ailing railroad workers at the nearby camp, the area became a resort, and was named **Ponce de Leon Springs**, after the elusive springs of eternal youth. It is not clear if anyone thought these springs were the authentic fountain of youth, but the waters were especially recommended for kidney diseases.

At one time Stone Mountain (sixteen miles away) could be seen from the resort. Near the springs was located a large hotel and a dancing platform. The springs themselves were situated at the bottom of a very steep hill, into which were built steps and walkways. A beautiful and restful parklike atmosphere was created, and the springs became a popular place for picnicking and courting, as well as for the medicinal and restorative powers. An amusement park and casino was built across the street from the springs.

In 1917, a great fire blackened Ponce between Parkway and Boulevard. Many buildings were dynamited during the fire to try to provide a firebreak.

In 1926, the **Sears Regional Catalogue Center** was built right on top of the old springs (675 Ponce). One story claims the water fountains inside still pump the old spring water; another story says the water is pumped straight into the Atlanta sewer system. A plaque on the side of the building commemorates the site. Today, the Sears Building has been taken over by the Atlanta Metro Police. The amusement park was redeveloped into the **Ponce de Leon Ball Park** for the Georgia Crackers baseball team, but that was torn down in 1967 and is now a parking lot.

Our tour of Ponce de Leon Avenue begins at the Fox Theatre, located at the intersection of Peachtree Street and Ponce.

**The Fox Theatre**, built in 1929 right after the infamous Stock Market Crash, is a magnificent creation. A tour is necessary to appreciate and savor all of the incredible intricacies, and tours can be made on Mondays, Thursdays, Saturdays, and Sundays, at 10:00 a.m. with the Atlanta History Center. Call 814-4000 for reservations. The Fox Theatre features interesting Egyptian motifs, including a 7,000 square foot ballroom with clerestory lighting (loosely based on the Temple of Karnac). One restroom emulates an Egyptian tomb with vaulted ceilings, and even includes a rug designed to evoke the waters of the Nile! Restrooms are available to be rented out for bridal showers or bachelor parties, but use your imagination and dream up another kind of bathroom bash! The theatre itself is reminiscent of a sultan's court on a midsummer's night in Persia, complete with 96 stars and special machines that make clouds float across the sky.

The whole theatre is a fantastical vision of what European culture imagined as the mysterious Orient. The decor adds combinations of Islamic and Art Deco design to the Egyptian motif, making this theatre an early (unintentional) example of Postmodernist Art and Architecture.

Tear yourself away from the Fox! There is so much more to see!

**The Georgian Terrace Hotel**, built in 1912, is located right across the street. Check out the swastika-decorated floors at the Georgian Terrace, which was the site of a gala celebration after the opening of Atlanta's most famous film, *Gone With the Wind*. Downstairs is another "must see," **The Road to Tara Museum**, which features memorabilia from the making of *Gone With the Wind*, including many wonderful photographs. There is also a gift shop next to the museum.

Behind the Georgian Terrace (on Ponce) was **The Copa**, an elegant nightclub where Jayne Mansfield and her husband Mickey Hargitay performed.

On the southeastern corner of Ponce and Peachtree Street stand the **Ponce de Leon Apartments**, built in 1913. The buildings feature two 4,000 square foot apartments, bachelor pads, and a roof garden. At one time, these two buildings were the tallest in Atlanta. In 1957, former debutante Mrs. Marion Gould committed suicide in her apartment by crawling into her refrigerator. She had to take out most of her food to do it; the food was found neatly stacked on the counter.

Finally, turn east on Ponce to begin the driving tour. Ponce de Leon Avenue is best seen at dusk, so as to properly appreciate all the wonderful neon decorating the Avenue.

At Piedmont (163 Ponce), see **The Abbey**, once a church, now a restaurant. Built in 1915, it was converted in 1968. **The Mansion** (179), built in 1885, was once part of a 400-acre tract belonging to the Peters family, early developers in Atlanta. It has been a restaurant since 1973. **Mary Mac's Tearoom** at 224 Ponce is a southern institution, well-loved for good cooking and a loyal staff.

Although **Little Tyrol** is one of the many sites that unfortunately can no longer be seen, we can't resist mentioning it. Once located between Piedmont and Myrtle, it was a lovely garden park with gazebo.

At the intersection of Ponce and Argonne, a Chinese teahouse and garden were located, built around 1885. Sadly, it too, is no longer standing. A John Waters-style Spaghetti Factory is at 249. Stop for hot frosted donuts at the **Krispy Kreme Donut Shop** (295), former home of the Pig n' Whistle Barbeque. While enjoying your donuts, watch others being made right before your eyes. Across the street is located the **Eagle Club**, a leather bar. Formerly the Celebrity Club, this was one of the main music bars of the early 80s. The club welcomed the Butthole Surfers, the Now Explosion, Ru "Star Booty" Paul, and Judy LaGrange, a psychic drag queen who could predict hurricanes.

Heading around the bend, don't miss the Shriner's temple on the left. For those of you on a food tour, **Popeye's** (on the right at Monroe) is a New Orleans-style fast food chicken joint. You need to ask if you want unsweetened iced tea.

Continuing along Ponce, check out the **Georgia Lighting display** on the left . . . two cinderblock structures on the street showcasing chandeliers and other exciting lighting products. **Zesto's**, also on the left at 544, is a re-creation of a

50s diner. It was actually open in the fifties, but was later remodeled to look more like the fifties.

Moving right along, check out the interesting looking old hotel apartments on the right, and the **Phoenix**, a hustler bar, also on the right. On the left is **Eats**, an excellent and very cheap place to eat. On the right, just past Eats, is the **Sears Building**, built over the infamous Ponce de Leon Springs, now City Hall East and a Metro Police Headquarters. Lee Haney's World Gym has also moved to this building. Check out the plaque located right on the front of the building by the steps. **The Georgia Crackers stadium, Spiller's Field**, was located right across the street from the Sears building. It was named after R.J. Spiller, owner of the park, and burned twice before it was abandoned. In the back of the field is an old magnolia tree. It was considered good luck to hit a ball into it. The last owner of the field even had his ashes scattered under this tree!

Continue down Ponce and go under the railroad bridge. This is were the original Yancey Spring was located. On the left, you can sometimes watch dogs being trained in the parking lot, and on the right, see the **Ford Factory Square**, which originally produced Model T Fords, beginning in 1915. Now on the National Register, the factory has been converted into apartments and first-floor commercial spaces. If you are still hungry after the hot frosted donuts, try a snack at **Tortilla's**, on the left at 752. Tortilla's is another excellent place to get large quantities of food for a very reasonable price. They specialize in burritos. On a summer evening, sit out on the deck to observe Common Nighthawks swooping across the sky. Across the street, at Green's liquor store, you can find everything for your alcoholic pleasure, including many of Ponce's most eclectic characters. Many more eccentric characters can be seen at the **Clermont Lounge and Hotel**, also on the right. The Clermont (aka Atlanta's Playboy Club and the Jungle Club) is where intensely debated and outrageous punk rocker G.G. Allen stayed while on a visit to Atlanta. Gary Krist and Ruth Eisemann-Schien, who kidnapped and buried alive heiress Barbara Jane Mackle, also stayed at the Clermont, in room 14-A. The lounge is well-known for their many unusual strip acts, including Blondie, a black stripper with blonde hair who crushes beer cans between her breasts.

**Jimmy Carter's new driveway** is next on the right. This is the very controversial new road to his Presidential Library. Out of respect to the many unhappy persons displaced by this roadway, we will recommend you take a different route to·the library (see chapter 4, Little Five Points).

So, passing up the new road, check out the old apartments on the left. **Fellini's** pizza is another good place for food, but surely, by now, you're totally stuffed. The Fellini's chain collects old neon; this Fellini's is good for their cheese and broccoli calzones. **The Majestic Diner, and the Plaza Theatre and Drug Store** heralds the end of our journey down Ponce de Leon. The Diner, open since 1938, is yet another good place to eat, but the decor alone is worth a visit, if only for coffee, and is open 24 hours a day, 7 days a week. YANKEES BEWARE! Please note: if you are getting up the courage to try the ubiquitous southern grits, DO NOT order them with milk and sugar. This is BAD! Very BAD! Classic grits are topped only with butter, salt, and pepper, and a Yankee had better not forget it, especially at the Majestic. An interesting bookstore, the Beaver Book Store (formerly a bowling alley), is located around the corner from the Majestic (in back of the diner). The Plaza Theatre, open since 1939, marks the end of the trip down Ponce. The Plaza opened with the constant dialogue film, *The Women.* It has had a career as a burlesque house in the 60s and a porno theatre in the 70s. Plaza Drugs, which once had a soda fountain, used its original 50s television commercials right up to the 80s. Check out the apartment building right across the street. Al Capone is rumored to have lived in this building; be sure to admire the architectural elements across the top.

Save this restaurant for later: **Soul Vegetarian II** is right around the corner at 652 North Highland. Continue down Highland a few more doors to check out the **Condom Art** condom store, the **Cafe Diem** (for desserts of a different vibration than hot donuts), and **Manuel's Tavern** (corner of North) where Atlanta's journalists and other literati hang out. It is also reputed to be one of Jimmy Carter's favorite haunts.

Once Ponce crosses Moreland (Briarcliff to the north), the complexion of the avenue changes radically. You have entered the **Druid Hills** neighborhood, home of Driving Miss Daisy (822 Lullwater), and site of massive displays of dogwood blossoms during the first week of April. Druid Hills was designed by Atlanta builder Joel Hurt, who also designed the Inman Park neighborhood. He was so enthusiastic about dogwoods that if one was in the way of construction, it would be dug up and replanted elsewhere. For all you persons not familiar with dogwoods, they grow wild only in this country, and in the fall their leaves turn red, providing another wonderful seasonal display. Many of the plantings alternate dogwood and sugar maple trees, which turn a lovely yellow in the fall. Druid Hills is an area of large, elegant homes and interesting gardens. The **Hare Krishnas** have a home and temple here (1287 Ponce), regularly staging services and festivals open to the public. The former mansion of **murdered Atlantan Henry Heinz** (1610) is now the Lullwater Estates, but much of the original facade remains. On the right is a deep ravine containing the **Cator-Woolford Gardens** at the Cerebral Palsy Center. This very serene spot is open to the public. For the Atlanta explorer, Druid Hills provides a nice, sharp contrast to the neon strip that is our driving tour of Ponce.

Just before Scott Boulevard splits off of Ponce (on your left), see the bridge famous for trucks getting wedged inside. If you are reading this as you drive, and are in a truck, move to the middle lane *right now!*

Ponce de Leon Avenue continues east through Decatur to **Stone Mountain**, going through two counties and five zip codes. The lowest point of Ponce is at the old springs (893 feet); the highest is 1060 feet at Hambrick Road in the town of Stone Mountain.

Inside the Fox Theatre

13

Inside Krispy Kreme

# A James Dean Date

**D**riving the neon glory of Ponce inspires us to suggest a quintessential James Dean date. Bring your sweetie, put on your best poodle skirt, and do up your hair! For dinner, we recommend **The Varsity**, established in 1928, located at 61 North Street (roughly in back of the Fox Theatre). Play your cards right, and you'll get a complimentary hat! Try the hotdogs, with everything. If you eat inside, head upstairs, where the atmosphere is reminiscent of eating in an airport restaurant. They call the style "Streamlined Moderne Meets the 60s." This is supposedly the oldest continually operated drive-in restaurant in the U.S. When Elvis was in Atlanta, he got take-out here.

Save room for dessert at **Zesto's** on Ponce (544). Try their chocolate malt with extra malt.

Turn right on Moreland and head south to the **Starlite Drive-In** for your choice of six different drive-in features. The neon is noteworthy in itself; you can't miss the place. The best lot is #4, where you can position your car to see three screens simultaneously. Sound is controlled through your car radio, so you can switch from one movie to another. The theatre opened in 1949 with one screen and a showing of the forgettable *The Inside Story*. Time your arrival early to watch the sun set over the city skyline. On hot summer nights, everyone sits outside their cars in the parking lot. You might bring lawn chairs, but if you sit on the pavement, keep an eye out for other cars so your legs don't get run over!

Later, go for a ride out to the **Federal Penitentiary** (continue south on Moreland, go right on McDonough Boulevard). The Pen, built in 1920, has walls two to four feet thick. Al Capone, Eugene V. Debs, and Nathanial Hawthorne's son Julian were among those housed here. The Prison Graveyard is located across the railroad tracks. Turn right again on Boulevard, cruise past **Grant Park and the Cyclorama**, and head north to Ponce.

# Chapter 4
# Little Five Points

(not to be confused with Five Points-Downtown)

Little Five Points is something of a puzzle. Described as the center of punk/counterculture/grunge activity in Atlanta, it is something of a contradiction. After all, Atlantans are so very friendly and polite, and even in Little Five Points this seems to hold true.

Little Five Points is a visit in itself; do not go early in the morning as nothing much opens before eleven. Once it does, and it does open slowly, the area is a warren of alternative shops, restaurants, bookstores, and more. Little Five Points is located around the intersection of Moreland and Euclid (from Ponce, head south on Moreland).

Check out the **Star Community Bar** (Hillbilly rock & roll), and **Baker's Cafe** (good breakfasts). **Crystal Blue** is a store specializing in crystals and other new age paraphernalia. Browse through the oddities at **Donna Van Gogh's Art for All o' Y'all**, and wander through the **A Capella Bookstore** (1133 Euclid). Located in the alley in back of the bookstore is **Blastoff Video**, run by the affable Sam Patton. Blastoff is the place to go for rare, obscure, and eclectic videos. Nowhere else in Atlanta can you find such a collection of psychotronic Hong Kong movies. **Princess Pamela's** is another place to find interesting items of popular culture. **Throb**, at 1140 Euclid, features fetish finery and lingerie. At **Junkman's Daughter** (464 Moreland), it is always Halloween. Next door is **Criminal Records** (music and comics). Natural foods, groceries, and other wholesome supplies can be found at **Sevenanda Natural Foods** (a community-owned grocery at 1111 Euclid Avenue). On the other side of Moreland at 1189 Euclid, be sure to check out **Charis**, a feminist bookstore which also has a very large selection of fine children's books.

Laden with reading material and other gifts and supplies,

it's time for lunch. **Eat Your Vegetables**, at 438 Moreland, serves tasty foccacias and other 90s fare. You would not go wrong with a meal at **La Fonda** (Cuban), the **Bridgetown Grille** (Jamaican), or **Fellini's** (which also houses good neon from the old Sans Souci lounge on West Peachtree).

Little Five Points is home to **Danny Beard's Wax and Fax**, the grand-daddy of all used record stores. Hear good music at **The Point**, a wedge-shaped building right in the center of Little Five Points.

Just south of Little Five Points, at Moreland, DeKalb, and Decatur (at the overpass) is where the painters must have stood and turned in a circle to create the Grant Park Cyclorama.

Just to the west is historic **Inman Park**, featuring lovely, restored Victorian homes. A visit to **Urban Nirvana** (15 Waddell Street, 1 mile west on DeKalb Avenue) will reveal treasures of the ceramic/garden ornament variety, but the Urban Nirvana decor alone is worth the trip. Nearby is a wonderful billboard, "My Mechanic is a Woman," advertising a woman-owned garage.

Boys burying fish heads discovered red gasoline spurting from the earth at McLendon and Clifton (east of L5P) in 1932. They eagerly dug sinkholes, filled fruit jars with the gas, and used it in their cars. Eventually, the bonanza was cut off, when it was discovered a nearby gas station had tanks leaking into the ground.

**Jimmy Carter's Presidential Library** is also in this area. It is located at 1 Copenhill Avenue, off Highland, which is where General Sherman stood to observe the Battle of Atlanta. We already mentioned the controversy surrounding the road to the center; the library itself is an absorbing place to visit. Housing permanent as well as temporary exhibits, the visitor can walk through the years of Carter's life and presidential tenure. There is a great deal of interactivity for even the casual visitor. Especially in the spring the landscaped grounds, which boast a view of the Atlanta skyline, are lovely. The park-like area is a good place to take a few moments to sit quietly and enjoy time passing by. The library also has a dining room, but we would recommend your returning to one of the more interesting eateries in Little Five Points, or to Soul Vegetarian II on Highland just south of Ponce.

Moreland Avenue continues south for many miles, eventually ending near Fort Gillem (a U.S. Military facility). South of route 20, Moreland boasts many unusually-named establish-

17

ments such as Hub Cap Daddy, Baby Tender, and Buffalo China. The Starlite Drive-In is a few miles further, on your left. As the skies darken, passages into the Drive-In, with its six theatre areas, light up like cattle chutes. Continue south on Moreland. The Federal Penitentiary is off to your right (spur 42, McDonough Boulevard).

Real southern treats are in store for the traveler who perseveres past route 285 (the loop around Atlanta). Here you might find your heart's fulfillment at **Charlie's**, home of the Daizey Duke contest. If you don't know who Daizey Duke was, go on in anyway, but play it smart. Daizey was a southern iconess on the *Dukes of Hazzard* TV show: very southern, very American, and very difficult to understand if you (a) aren't from the south, or (b) never saw the show. Suffice it to say, the lady is a quintessential expression of southern redneckism. By all means, go in, really!

Next door to Charlie's is the **Rio Bravo**, offering "Catfish and Hush Puppies, No Beer." More classic southern iconography here but why no beer? We like Moreland Avenue because it travels through so many phases of our American culture: punk to prisoners, drive-ins to drive-by shootings, catfish to Carter; there it is. It is a microcosm of America seen along one road, from the relative safety and comfort of your own automobile.

Sam Patton at Blastoff Video

18

Southview Cemetery

Atlanta Trailer City

19

# Chapter 5
# A Connecting Drive

**T**his drive connects Moreland and the Starlite Drive-In to the West End, or you can circle back to Grant Park and Cabbagetown. From Moreland, head west on McDonough Boulevard (spur 42) to pass by **the Federal Penitentiary**. This structure, built in 1902, boasts its own "great wall." The wall is 4,178 feet long, up to four feet thick, and 37 feet high. Al Capone, Socialist and Presidential Candidate Eugene Debs, and Nathaniel Hawthorne's son Julian all spent time here. It was the scene of several notorious escape attempts. Dutch Anderson tunneled out and vanished, but later shot a cop in Michigan, who then rose up to kill him. Gerald Chapman did escape from the second floor infirmary by lowering himself with tied sheets. He was eventually caught and shot, but escaped from an Athens hospital. In 1926, he was finally hanged in Connecticut for the murder of a police officer.

The prison garden was the site of a possible UFO crash in 1960. The object shooting through the sky was clearly seen by several people, but the military claimed it was a test bomb (unloaded) that had fallen from a training plane, despite reports by observers who had seen the object coming in almost horizontally over their houses.

Turn left on Sawtell, right on Jonesboro Road (route 54) to visit **Southview Cemetery** where the Reverend Martin Luther King, Jr. was originally buried and where his parents still rest. There is also a large ex-slave graveyard here.

Head back up route 54 to Sawtell and turn left (the road changes to Claire). Bear left at the fork onto Lakewood Avenue into **Lakewood Park**. Lakewood once boasted a mountain. During the depression, WPA crews blew it up and hauled it away. Lakewood also featured a racetrack, movie studio, and amusement park. The park's roller coaster was blown up by Jackie Gleason, playing Buford T. Justice, for

*Smokey and the Bandit II.* Lakewood now centers much of its activity on a flea market the second Tuesday of every month. Concerts are still held in the Lakewood Amphitheatre, and great old buildings still stand in the park.

Return to Lakewood Avenue and drive west again. Lakewood will become the Lakewood Freeway. You will want to head north on route 3 (Stewart Avenue).

**Stewart Avenue**, one of Atlanta's original "miracle miles," is a good place to look for outstanding hairdos on a Saturday afternoon. Look also for interesting examples of 1950s art and architecture as you cruise up the strip.

In 1981, scandal swept Stewart when over 200 porn photos involving 53 children were seized in a Stewart Avenue motel.

The Gold Rush Showbar and Strip Joint, featuring five-dollar table dances, once hosted strippers Kid Natividad and Pattey Plenty in a special appearance. A former owner was murdered by an (alleged) corrupt cop burglary ring. At 2370 Stewart (on your right) is the former Alamo Plaza & Hotel Courts, now a halfway house. The Alamo was once host to a pre-wedding bachelor party murder: a drug deal gone bad. You will also pass the Atlanta Trailer City and FunTown Amusement Center & Bowl. The bowling alleys are still open, but FunTown has been taken over by the dreaded kudzu vine.

At 1650, the Oaks Motor Court reputedly houses prostitute activity. There is a museum in the Salvation Army College. A squadron of old planes is grounded in back of the Atlanta Technical School. Mrs. Winner's, a chicken restaurant at University, is a good place to order a breast substitution. It's especially fun to do this at the drive-thru window (there's a 13 year old boy in all of us!).

Just east of University on McDaniel is the site of the outbreak of the infamous **Pittsburg riot** of 1902. The Pittsburg neighborhood stretches from Stewart to the railroad tracks, and from University roughly to Ralph D. Abernathy Blvd.

North of University turn right on Rockwell to see **Bailey's Sculpture Garden** at 396. E.M. Bailey's backyard monuments and shrines are plaster figures commemorating Hank Aaron, JFK, and dancing muses, to name a few.

**At this juncture, you might want to head east on University to explore the Cabbagetown/Grant Park area, or continue north on Stewart and west on Ralph D. Abernathy Boulevard to check out the West End.**

Funtown, Stewart Avenue

Town & Country, Stewart Avenue

Oakland Cemetery, with Cabbagetown in the background

Wall at Oakland Cemetery

# Chapter 6
# Cabbagetown & Its Environs

**A** neighborhood created to house workers at the now defunct Fulton Bag & Cotton Mill, Cabbagetown is said to have found its name after a cabbage truck accidentally turned over on one of the streets. Now a Historic District, Cabbagetown is bounded on the north by the railroad tracks and the mill, to the west by Boulevard and Oakland Cemetery, and to the south by Memorial Drive. **The Fulton Bag & Cotton Mill** was founded in 1881 by German Jacob Elsas who came to Atlanta after the War. (There was only one war for Atlanta!) It became a center for union organizing activity in the 1930s, but the first strike held there was in 1897, to protest the hiring of blacks.

Organizing attempts in 1932 by 19-year-old communist recruiter Angelo Herndon resulted in his conviction for insurrection. He was sentenced to 18 to 20 years. A National Textile Strike in 1934 put the Fulton Bag & Cotton Mill in the center of radical political activity. An earlier attempt to organize Atlanta Industrial Workers resulted in the Atlanta 6, two women, two black men, and two white men (Mod Squad x 2) being charged with "attempting to incite insurrection." The Supreme Court, in 1937, threw out the anti-insurrection laws, ruling they violated Constitutional rights to free speech and assembly.

Some of the film *Kalifornia* was made here in the Fulton Bag and Cotton Mill disguised as a Pittsburgh (PA) factory. Brad Pitt, as "Early Grace," also threw a brick from the near-by bridge over Boulevard.

Threats to Cabbagetown still come from the Fulton Bag & Cotton Mill as developers seek to turn the old mill into lofts, "revitalize" the historic neighborhood, drive up property values, and drive out the original neighbors. This is the "Cabbagetown Empowerment Plan" of 1995.

Traveling west on Memorial Drive, cross Boulevard and

you are at the southeast corner of **Oakland Cemetery**, one of the richest in Atlanta both historically and aesthetically. Nearby, just south of the corner of Memorial and Park, is the spot where several of **Andrew's Raiders** were hanged. A plaque inside the cemetery describes the event.

Return to Boulevard and drive south to **Grant Park**, which will be on your left. The neighborhood around Grant Park, also called Grant Park, is on the National Register and is worth time spent to admire restored homes of many styles, from Victorian to Craftsman bungalows. The southwest corner of Grant Park was once the site of **"Little Switzerland,"** an exclusive park built in the style of a beer garden by a German landscape artist. Also known as "White City," Little Switzerland boasted "all objectionable parties are excluded." The Park itself is home to **Zoo Atlanta** and the quintessential **Cyclorama**, one of the absolute "must sees" in this city. The Zoo was created in 1889 when two men, G.V. Gress and Thomas J. James, bought a stranded circus for $4,500. Donated to Grant Park were the nineteen animals, including a raccoon!

For many years, another zoo existed in Atlanta. Buddie Candler, son of Coca-Cola magnate Asa Candler, Sr., bought a circus on a visit to Eastern Europe. A zoo was built in the front yard of his home at 1260 Briarcliff Road, now the DeKalb Addiction Clinic. When it arrived, the five elephants (named Delicious, Refreshing, Coca, Cola, and Rosa) hooked trunks to tails and paraded through the streets of Druid Hills to their new home. Enthusiastic about his project, Buddie added lions, horses, and monkeys to his Briarcliff Zoological Gardens. Neighbors complained the lions kept them awake at night with their roaring. Animals often escaped and wandered the streets, terrorizing the neighborhood. Candler eventually bowed to public pressure and donated his animals to the Atlanta Public Zoo.

The zoo had many problems, not the least of which was Willie B., a gorilla, who in 1935 escaped and chased a woman down the street. Willie B. ran for 5th District Congressman in 1960, earning 663 votes. Zoo Atlanta was rocked with scandal in the 1980s when reports surfaced of animals being sold to workers for food, of a sick elephant being given to a circus shortly before it died, and of the prairie dog town accidentally being cemented over with the little rodents inside.

G.V. Gress also gave the Cyclorama to Grant Park. The Cyclorama, donated in 1893, was bought by him (slightly damaged) for $1,100. The Cyclorama is a detailed rendering (somewhat whimsical) of the Battle of Atlanta, painted by over a dozen German artists. The actual viewpoint for the Cyclorama is on the overpass at Moreland, DeKalb, and Decatur. The painting is 42 feet high and 358 feet around, and is simply magnificent. Call 624-1071 for information.

# Snakepit

Olivia de Havilland, best known for her portrayal of the quintessentially perfect blossom of southern womanhood in the film *Gone With the Wind*, also starred in the terrifying *Snake Pit*, a 1948 movie set in a mental institution.

**The Atlanta Stockade**, at 750 Glenwood Avenue, is Atlanta's own version of the Snakepit. A debtor's prison built in 1887, it now houses 67 efficiency apartments. The stockade (Glen Castle), still inspires rumors and urban legends of women being hanged from the rafters, and of slave containers (not coffins) half buried in the grounds outside. The building was empty for many years, and reports of daredevils rapelling from inside the towers were heard. The old school building right next door (built to educate the children of the women prisoners), is filled with artists' studios and galleries. It is, in itself, worth a visit. Take Interstate 20 east to exit 26 (Boulevard/Cyclorama). Go left almost immediately on Glenwood, and another left at the second street (Cameron), which becomes Kalb. The Stockade will be on your left. To check on exhibitions and hours, call 624-4211.

# Chapter 7
# The War of Northern Aggression

**N**ow, is there anyone who truly does not know what war we are talking about? Issues surrounding the Civil War (as it is known to Yankees) or the War Between the States (the most neutral designation) are not yet resolved, even with the passage of more than 100 years time. In many parts of the South, this war was fought just yesterday, and anger still seethes, usually just under the surface. But not too far, and it tends to come bursting out where you least expect it.

Why is there still anger? While we in the home office of *Sideways Atlanta* would not presume to speak for the disenfranchised, we offer one explanation. When asked, many Southerners will say, "Slavery was not the issue; we were fighting for our way of life." The idea is that slave culture was a very small part of the whole picture, and that all southerners had to pay for the practices of a few rich white men. While certainly plausible, it still does not answer the question. What exactly, then, was the way of life they were fighting for?

Nonetheless, tempers still rage over the Yankee outrages committed during this time; battles are constantly refought. The old cry, "The South Shall Rise Again," is a widespread belief throughout the region. People who complain too much about these attitudes are told: "Delta's ready when you are!" Or, "I-75 goes both ways!"

One name will inflame more passion than all the others put together, and that is the name of **General William Tecumseh Sherman**. Sherman fought the Confederates back from Chattanooga to Atlanta, occupied Atlanta for several months, then burned it to the ground before marching on to the sea (Savannah). It is Sherman's route we will retrace for you on your Confederate Tour of Atlanta.

Sherman's **"Atlanta Campaign"** began in Chattanooga, Tennessee during the very cold winter of 1864. In early May, with 100,000 men, the march of Northern troops into Georgia commenced. Confederate General Joseph E. Johnston, at Dalton, had but 50,000 men to hold back the Union forces.

We will begin our tour at the **Confederama**, located in the shadow of Lookout Mountain, on the south side of Chattanooga, Tennessee. The Confederama, now known by the gentler name of "The Battle of Chattanooga," recreates, from a distinctly Confederate perspective, the battles of Lookout Mountain, Chickamauga, and Chattanooga. The battles take place on a large horizontal relief map laid out in a darkened room, with flashing twinkle lights representing the troops in action. It is really quite an exciting presentation, especially if you are lucky enough to have some actual live Confederates in the room with you (in our case, they were three 75+ year-old ladies, with spunk). Our ladies enthusiastically cheered the valiant boys in grey, hissing and spitting whenever Yankees (especially Sherman) were mentioned! Afterwards, cool down by visiting the gift shop for mementos of this heart-in-mouth experience.

If you have time, take the very scary incline railroad up the side of **Lookout Mountain** to visit the small museum at the top. Be sure to walk down to the lookout for a spectacular view of the Tennessee River and marvel at how anyone could have pushed heavy cannons and other military equipment up the sides of the mountain. See our chapter on Out of Town Trips for a few other interesting things to do in Chattanooga. We recommend your saving the Confederama for last, so you can be all pumped up as you head south on route 75 toward Atlanta, just the way Sherman did in May of 1864.

**Dalton, Resaca, Adairsville** . . . Sherman marched almost directly along the route that Interstate 75 now takes. There are still many places where one might find bullets and other remnants of those battles. In early June, Sherman seized **Big Shanty** (now Kennesaw). Near Big Shanty the **New Manchester Manufacturing Company** (a cotton mill) and the dam across **Sweetwater Creek** were destroyed.

From Big Shanty, Sherman went on to fight battles at Kennesaw Mountain and Cheatham's Hill, located in what is now the **Kennesaw Mountain National Battlefield Park**, just west of Marietta. Using his now-famous "flanking technique," Sherman squeezed the outnumbered Confederates, pushing them further and further south towards Atlanta. By July, Sherman could write, "Atlanta is in plain view," as he ordered his men to arrest all civilians and ship the women north, across the Ohio River. On July 17, he crossed the

Chattahoochee River at Powers Ferry to begin his capture and occupation of Atlanta.

Meanwhile, the Confederates had switched Generals from Johnston to Hood, also known as "Old Pegleg." The headquarters were located at the Niles House, 1030-1042 West Marietta Street, near the railroad yards. Sherman, headquartered in Vinings, Georgia before he crossed the Chattahoochee, relocated at the Samuel House residence at the corner of Peachtree & Old Cross Keys Road (now the Peachtree Golf Club). At the same time Yankees were positioned at Stone Mountain under the lead of Generals McPherson and Garrard.

**The Battle of Peachtree Creek** began on July 20th; a monument is located on Peachtree Road, opposite Brighton. With Sherman now headquartered at the northwest intersection of North Decatur and Briarcliff, other troops headed into the city from Decatur along the railroad, resting for the night at the intersection of Moreland and Flat Shoals, just south of route 20 (Bald Hill, now known as Leggett's Hill).

**The Battle of Atlanta** commenced on the 22nd of July at the intersection of Memorial and Clay, overlooking Sugar Creek, continuing to Leggett's Hill. General Sherman watched from atop a hill, now the site of the Jimmy Carter Presidential Center. General Hood's headquarters were located opposite Oakland Cemetery between Boulevard and Yonge.

The Battle of Atlanta is best enjoyed by a trip to the **Cyclorama**, located in Grant Park, south of Interstate route 20 along Boulevard. The Battle can be relived fifteen times a day from a revolving platform overlooking a 358-foot long, 42-foot high circular painting depicting the battle. The painting itself was completed in 1886 by a group of European artists. It was set into its current building in 1921, and during the 1930s the battle was made three-dimensional by adding figures, landscape, railroad tracks, and other battle equipment to the area in front of the painting. Your headquarters for the Atlanta Civil War experience, the Cyclorama building also houses an excellent museum, a very satisfying (if small) bookstore, and the companion locomotive used in the infamous Andrew's Raid, the "Texas." A visit to the Cyclorama will give you a good base from which to look for the actual spots around town.

General McPherson died during the battle, and a monument to his heroism can be found at the corner of McPherson and Monument. A monument to Confederate General Walker, who also died, is located at Wilkinson Drive and Glenwood

Avenue.   The Cyclorama depicts much fighting around the Hurt House, 191 DeGress Avenue, now the site of the East Atlanta Primitive Baptist Church.

By July 28, fighting had moved to the west side of town, and a battle was fought at **Ezra Church**, in and around Westview Cemetery where Anderson Avenue connects to Ralph D. Abernathy.

By August, residents were fleeing Atlanta.  Sherman was camped north of Westview Cemetery at Bankhead Highway and Chapel Road.

Heavy shelling on August 10 resulted in the death of Negro barber Solomon Luckie.  He was struck at the corner of Whitehall and Alabama, where the shell lodged in a lamppost, one of the first fifty lit in Atlanta at Christmas, 1855.   Until 1880 the lamppost was kept in City Hall, when it was moved to its original site, now at the bottom of the stairs at the entranceway of Underground Atlanta.  In 1919 it was dedicated to the memory of General A.J. West, a Confederate veteran from Atlanta by the United Daughters of the Confederacy.  In December of 1939, for the premiere of *Gone With the Wind*, the lamp was lighted with gas, courtesy of the Atlanta Gas & Light Company . . . "the Eternal Flame of the Confederacy."

By the end of August, Sherman ended his siege in order to move south to draw General Hood away from the city.  After the August 25 battle of Jonesboro, Hood gave orders for his troops to evacuate Atlanta, but not before blowing up his own ammunition depots.  The remnants of the Confederate Army headed south, out of town, on Capitol Avenue.  General Slocum was on his way in via Bankhead Highway, and on September 2, Mayor of Atlanta James M. Calhoun, accompanied by a group of men, surrendered the city to the Yankees. Starting at Five Points, Calhoun made his way west looking for someone to surrender to.  General Hood could not participate in this sad duty since he was busy chasing General Sherman.  Finally, at Marietta and Northside, Calhoun and his men found Colonel John Coburn (Yankee) who made them surrender the city via a formal note to General Sherman which he promised to pass on when next he saw the General.

Finally, Sherman and the armies of the north occupied Atlanta.  Headquartered at what are now the grounds of City Hall, he made no effort to halt the looting.  He claimed, "all cotton is tainted with treason, and no title in it will be respected."  All citizens were ordered to evacuate the city on September 5.  The refugees would go to the town of Rough and Ready, now no longer in existence, but then some ten miles north of Jonesboro (along Jonesboro Road in the vicinity of Southview Cemetery and Lakewood Park). Central headquarters for the refugees was at the Rough and Ready Tavern, located on what is now the Old Dixie Highway near the airport. The Old Dixie Highway (routes 19/41) is a continuation of Stewart Avenue. A plaque marks the site of the tavern; it is near the county line by a used-car lot.

Meanwhile, Hood made some final attempts to draw Sherman out of the city, but ended up heading through Alabama into Tennessee. Sherman decided to drop pursuit of Hood and began his infamous march across Georgia to the sea.

With 63,000 men, Sherman's march commenced in mid-November. It was at this time he set fire to the city of Atlanta and burned it to the ground. Two groups of troops headed out. One group went south, towards Jonesboro. The other, led by General Sherman, marched east by way of Decatur Street to Lithonia, where he camped with Stone Mountain in plain view. Both armies were headed for Milledgeville, the capital of Georgia, before heading on to Savannah and the sea.

**The Burning of Atlanta** left a deserted, devastated city. The city treasury held one dollar and sixty-four cents. By December 15, 1864, however, Atlanta was starting to rebuild. Already there was a grocery, bar, barber, post office, and a newspaper, the *Intelligencer*. Thousands of dogs and cats roamed the city. Citizens roamed with them, looking for scraps of materials with which to rebuild their lives.

A complete trip through Atlanta's part in the War Between the States might take days. A serious historian could spend hours at each of the many battlefields; a whole day could be spent in Chattanooga or at Kennesaw Mountain. Nevertheless, we will outline a route retracing Sherman's path of destruction:

Begin at the Confederama, in the shadow of Lookout Mountain in Chattanooga, Tennessee. From route 75 north take route 24 west to Cummings Highway (routes 64/72). Go south to route 17. Look for the incline railroad on the side of the mountain; the Confederama ("The Battle of Chattanooga") is right around the corner. When finished, turn and head south again on route 75. If you want to travel closer to the actual path of Sherman, get on route 41, just south of the state line. Either way, you will pass by Dalton, Resaca, and Adairsville before arriving in Kennesaw. The Kennesaw Mountain Battlefield is just west of Marietta. Sweetwater Creek State Park, south of I-20 is near exit 12 (west of Atlanta). Ruins of the old factory still stand. From route 41 you can take Paces Mill Road (just before crossing the Chattahoochee) to get to Vinings, where Sherman stood poised to make his entry into Atlanta.

Sherman entered Atlanta at Powers Ferry. From route 41 south of the Galleria, take Akers Mill Road northeast to where it runs into Powers Ferry Road. Cross the river, go right on Northside, and left on Mt. Vernon Highway to Old Powers Ferry Road. Go right, head south to West Wieuca and go right. At Peachtree turn left, and head for 4600 (at Old Cross Keys Road). Sherman next headquartered at North Decatur and Briarcliff, which can be reached by heading back down Peachtree to North Druid Hills Road. Turn left, and at Briarcliff, turn right. This will be soon after you pass under Interstate 85. From Briarcliff and North Decatur, you can head south (Briarcliff will turn into Moreland). At Euclid, go to the Carter Presidential Center, where Sherman watched the Battle of Atlanta. Highland will take you west to Boulevard. Go south on Boulevard to Grant Park, home of the Atlanta Cyclorama.

Confederama (The Battle of Chattanooga)

Surrender of Atlanta,
intersection of Marietta and Northside Streets

# Where was Scarlett?

Scores of fans scour Atlanta each year searching for places made familiar by Margaret Mitchell in her epic novel, *Gone With the Wind.* Here is a blow-by-blow account of Scarlett O'Hara's activities during the nightmarish siege of Atlanta.

Melanie Wilkes (sweet, gentle wife of the noble Ashley) is pregnant. Scarlett, blinded by love for Ashley, foolishly promises to take care of Melanie, no matter what. So, despite turmoil in the city, exorbitant prices, mud, and audible sounds of battle, Scarlett stays with Melanie, who is too delicate to be moved. Even news of fighting around Jonesboro (near her beloved Tara), and reports of her family stricken with typhoid do not dislodge Scarlett.

She wants to go. She is desperate to go. She can't believe she made such a stupid promise to Ashley, but she did and now she's stuck.

On September 1, Melanie is in labor. This is the day General Hood orders his troops to abandon Atlanta and blow up the ammunition depots. Scarlett unsuccessfully looks for help among doctors tending the wounded at Five Points, racing back up Peachtree to deliver the baby with the help of the maid Prissy. Scarlett lived somewhere north of Wesley Chapel on Peachtree. (Originally, the Wesley Chapel was located where the Candler Building is now, near the Atlanta Public Library and the site of the Loew's Theatre, where *Gone With the Wind* premiered.) With the baby (finally) born, Scarlett knows they must leave town. Everything is on fire, not due to Sherman, but to the Confederates themselves. She enlists the aid of the roguish but sensual Captain Rhett Butler and heads south out of town via Capitol Avenue, the main road to Rough and Ready (Capitol eventually becomes Jonesboro Road). In the decrepit wagon are Melanie, the baby, Prissy, and Scarlett's young son, Wade. The odious Captain Butler leaves them once they get clear of the city, to join the Confederate Army! By the morning of September 2, Scarlett and her ragtag party are about 15 miles from Tara on the back road to Rough and Ready. In Atlanta, Mayor Calhoun has surrendered the city to the Yankees. General Sherman was involved in the Battle of Jonesboro, south of the city on Macon Road near East Point, placing him several miles west of Scarlett, who arrived home at dusk to find Tara whole but her mother dead.

"The Dump," where Margaret Mitchell wrote
*Gone With the Wind*

Corner of Memorial and Park
where seven of the Andrews Raiders were hanged

# Andrews Raiders

April 12, 1862 marked a daring event in the story of the Civil War. James J. Andrews (from Kentucky) was selected to lead 22 Federal men in a raid against the railway between Atlanta and Chattanooga. The purpose was to sever the connection between the two Confederate cities, and hasten the end of the war.

The group (except for two who overslept) met and boarded the train in Marietta. The plan was to steal the locomotive the "General" in Big Shanty (now Kennesaw), by separating the engine and several cars from the train when everyone left to eat breakfast. With that accomplished, the raiders took off, pursued by engineers on foot. Once they realized they were not chasing deserters, but Federal spies, the men got a push car, then another engine, the "Yonah," and yet another, the "William R. Smith." When the raiders removed rails from the track, the pursuers found another engine, the "Texas." Unfortunately, the "Texas" was headed in the wrong direction, so the men simply started chasing backwards.

With the "Texas" in hot pursuit, the "General" had less time to stop and disable the tracks. Finally, the "General" ran out of steam about two miles north of Ringgold and died. Andrews and his Raiders took to the woods but everyone was captured.

James J. Andrews was executed on June 7, 1862 about 50' southeast of the intersection of Juniper and Third. With his legs still chained, he was buried without a coffin under a nearby pine tree. On June 18, seven more of the Raiders were hanged, this time at Memorial and Park. A plaque is located inside Oakland Cemetery where Park joins Memorial Drive. All of the Raiders, including Andrews himself, were later moved to the National Cemetery at Chattanooga where they are buried surrounding a bronze replica of the "General."

Eight remaining Raiders eventually escaped, and six were exchanged as prisoners of war. The "General" is now located at the Big Shanty Museum in Kennesaw. The "Texas" is on display at the Cyclorama. The General, a 1926 film starring Buster Keaton, told the whole story.

# Chapter 8
# Reconstruction

The seven years immediately following the War were difficult for Atlanta and all of Georgia as people began the work of putting their lives back in order. In 1865, all Confederate money was useless and prices were high: five dollars per pound for bacon, six dollars per dozen for eggs, twenty dollars per bushel for potatoes. There was plenty of everything, if you had the money.

Displaced Atlantans quickly returned to rebuild their city. Unfortunately, on their heels came thousands of newly freed slaves looking for a new life, and scores of entrepreneurs from the North, looking for profit. More than 60,000 fatherless children and orphans needed some means of survival.

Atlanta was a military post run by Yankees and commanded, for a time, by a **German prince, Prince Felix Salm-Salm**. The army distributed food, attracting thousands to the city, but stopped mid-winter, causing even more hardship. Crime was rampant and escalating out of control. Neighborhoods of shacks were hastily built, with many, such as Tight Squeeze at 10th & Peachtree, becoming notorious for their criminal activities. In 1866 a smallpox epidemic broke out, hitting hardest the poverty stricken and starving former slave population.

**The Reconstruction Act of 1867** did little to help. Resumption of military control, the Negro right to vote, and forced registration of voters did not set well with Atlantans. The act also included a law which made it extremely difficult for anti-reconstruction newspapers to be printed. Nonetheless, most people felt the world would eventually right itself with white supremacy again at the top of the heap.

**Atlanta University** was chartered in 1867, the first of the six colleges for Negroes in the city of Atlanta. The same year saw the **first Orthodox Jewish Temple** (on the SE corner of Grant & Forsyth), the **first Library** (Alabama Street), the **first**

**soda fountain** (Whitehall & Alabama at the Redwine & Fox Drug Store), and the building of the **original Rich's Department Store** at 36 Whitehall. **The Atlantic Brewery** (Courtland & Harris) was also founded. A lottery to help the 60,000 orphans and fatherless children was created; it continued until 1877.

1867 was the year of the **Grand Ladies Fair**, a special event to raise money for the Fire Company. Graced by a life-sized candy bell, the fair held an unusual contest (for the time). The lady receiving the most votes would have the new fire engine named after her. The runner-up would have her name engraved on the fire alarm bell. The winner, Miss Emma Latimer, decided it would be unladylike to name an engine after her, so the truck became "Castalia." Miss Augusta Hill, presumably less sensitive, did have her name engraved on the 1,995 pound bell that sat atop the fire house at Broad Street and the railroad tracks, ringing for fires and on the day Miss Hill died. The bell now sits on the ground at Engine House #1 by Markham, Techwood, and Chapel (just east of Atlanta University), and near the old Snake Nation.

Politically, life in Atlanta continued to deteriorate. **The 1868 Constitutional Convention** was attended by Negroes, Carpetbaggers (opportunists from the North), and Scalawags (opportunists from the South). A dozen conservative whites managed to get themselves in. And although the KKK worked hard to prevent blacks from voting, the ratification election outlawed whipping, required a free education system be created, gave married women full rights of property, and held women not liable for their husband's debts. Scarlett must have been happy that day!

When military rule ended (as a result of the ratification), the Legislature immediately expelled all Negro members. The state was promptly put back under military rule by the federal government, who declared Georgia would not be readmitted to the union until the 15th Amendment, giving male Negroes the right to vote, was ratified.

An incident in the 4th Ward at the corner of Gilmer & Pratt illustrated the problem of forced reconstruction. Carousing peacemakers (federal soldiers) rioted against the control and authority of four local policemen. Happily, the policemen won, quelling the disturbance without loss of life.

On the plus side, Reconstruction helped shift Georgia's power structure away from plantations. Small towns with small support businesses were created, and Atlanta became the shipping and distribution center for goods flowing in and out of the region.

**Humbug Square** was located near the railroad station in an area left vacant by the burning of Atlanta. Attracting visiting out-of-towners in particular, the Square featured disreputable vendors, magicians, con artists, and medicine shows. Today, Underground Atlanta sits on the site of Humbug Square.

Healing from the War proceeded slowly. The first **Confederate Memorial Day** was held on April 26, 1866, date of Johnston's surrender to Sherman in 1865. The day was commemorated by moving Confederate soldiers from hastily dug burial trenches to more dignified resting places in Oakland Cemetery. Confederate Memorial Day is still celebrated on April 26.

In 1869 Governor Rufus Bullock (a Scalawag from Augusta, Georgia) forced the legislature to adopt the 15th Amendment so Georgia could become a state again. It was something of a dilemma: Georgia couldn't be a state until the amendment passed, but did not have the power to ratify the amendment if it wasn't a state. Nonetheless, it was done. Then, by forcing all legislators to swear (under oath) they had not been part of the "rebellion," the governor was able to oust enough conservative whites to stay in power. The new state owned all the railroads, and Governor Bullock promptly put them to good use by floating bond issues to pay for his numerous expenses and political appointees.

An interesting relationship existed between Bullock and **Hannibal Ingalls Kimball**, financier. Originally from Maine, Kimball arrived in Atlanta in 1867, looking for profit. He found it in his association with Governor Bullock, who allowed him to make ample use of the railroad resources. Kimball became a close advisor to Bullock, but tried to avoid direct participation in politics, for "business" reasons. From the sidelines, Kimball financed *The New Era* newspaper, which gave Bullock and his supporters a voice. Chiefly known for harsh attacks on the conservative faction, it folded in 1872 when both Kimball and Bullock abruptly left the state.

Kimball was responsible for buying the Atlanta Opera House to rebuild as the State Capitol, for building the **Kimball House**, a $600,000 luxury hotel on Pryor, and for selling both before completion in the wake of financial troubles and accusations of corrupt behavior. Kimball had many troubles. He had great ideas for improvements to Atlanta, and was instrumental in organizing the **first Georgia State**

**Fair** at Oglethorpe Park in 1870, for re-opening Oglethorpe University, and creating the first women's college, among many other important enterprises. It's just that his bankruptcy in 1871 totalled liabilities of $5,000,000, and he was accused of depositing state monies in his own account for use in private financial projects. Many allegations were made accusing Bullock and Kimball of being "partners in corruption."

Indictments were made at various times on a variety of charges, yet due to the death of witnesses and confusing testimonies, Bullock was acquitted and Kimball was found innocent by association.

Kimball returned to Atlanta to help start a cotton factory which encountered financial problems, not the least of which was Kimball using company coal at his own house (located where the Fox Theatre is now). Eventually the mill opened, with ex-Governor Bullock as president. Kimball went on to run for mayor in 1880, and organized the **International Cotton Exposition** held in 1881 in Oglethorpe Park, but left again because "Atlanta could not meet up to my expectations." He turned up once more a year later when the Kimball House burned to the ground (1883). The fire was started by the cigar of an Italian lemon dealer. Kimball vowed to rebuild, almost immediately experiencing financial difficulty. After it was finally completed, Kimball moved in with his family. The new hotel, on Pryor Street near the Union Depot, was larger than the original and was fireproof. He then turned to the task of organizing conventions, and set Atlanta on the road to becoming a convention city. He was also responsible for helping establish the West View Cemetery, participated in the Temperance Movement, and had a hand in several failed land development groups. He left Atlanta for good in 1886, going on to develop Kimball City near Lookout Mountain, Tennessee. That company eventually went bankrupt. H.I. Kimball died in 1895 and was buried in Brooklyn, New York.

Reconstruction in Georgia officially ended with the departure of Governor Rufus B. Bullock and the election in 1872 of Democrat James Smith. Recovery in Georgia officially continues to this day.

# Chapter 9
# Margaret Mitchell

**D**evotees of Margaret Mitchell's epic novel of the War Between the States and its aftermath are often shocked to discover that, while based on fact, the characters and places are total fiction. There is no Tara. There was no Rhett Butler. No Scarlett. No Belle Watling's House of Ill Repute. If Scarlett's prosperous post-Civil War lumberyard was at 5 Points; it has obviously fallen prey to urban renewal!

The city abounds however, with *Gone With the Wind* movie memorabilia, and the tourist can still visit some of the areas where Margaret Mitchell lived and worked.

Mitchell was born in 1900, and spent her early childhood on **Jackson Street**, near Cain, just five blocks north of the Ebenezer Baptist Church on Auburn Avenue. Her home, however, was among the many later destroyed in the great fire of 1917. Margaret, while on Jackson, lived through the riots of 1906, helping her father, armed with an ax and a sword, guard their house.

Margaret grew up on **Peachtree Street**, near Ansley Park. As a teenager, she staged a version of the notorious film *Birth of a Nation*, and won a prize from the United Daughters of the Confederacy for a paper that turned out to be plagiarized. During her brief time as a student at Smith College in Massachusetts, she refused to stay in a class with a Negro woman student. **Yankees made Margaret very nervous**, and she quickly returned to Atlanta.

Debutante activities at the Capital City Club and the Piedmont Driving Club coincided both with the outbreak of World War I and the great fire of 1917. Margaret, who made her debut during the 1920-21 season, was known as a gifted conversationalist and a charming raconteur. In 1923, in the throes of a failing marriage, Mitchell took up a career in journalism, attracted by the seamier aspects: the drinking, swearing, and carousing. She began working for the *Atlanta*

*Journal* in the magazine section.  She got the job by lying about her past experience and her typing skills.  Nonetheless, she worked very hard, producing articles such as "Where Women Still Use Curl Papers" (1924), and "Atlanta Sub Debs Pass Up Tutankamen" (1928).  She continued to write short stories, outlined several never-finished novels, and began *Gone With the Wind* around 1926.

At the time Margaret and her husband John Marsh lived in **The Dump** (1925-32), located at the corner of Peachtree and Tenth.  The Dump, also known as the Windsor House Apartments, was designated as the **Margaret Mitchell Historical Landmark.**  It mysteriously burned in 1994, but is being rebuilt for the Olympics.  Mitchell also lived in basement apartment #1 at the corner of South Prado and Piedmont, in Ansley Park.  There is a commemorative plaque on this building.  Rumor has it, Mitchell burned some of her manuscripts here.

**Opening night** for the film in 1939 was at the Loew's Theatre with a ball afterward at the Georgian Terrace (NE corner of Peachtree and Ponce).  Blacks were dressed up as slaves to perform spirituals, including Martin Luther King, Jr., age 10, with his mother at the organ.  Other blacks, even the actors and actresses themselves, were not allowed to attend; they held another celebration at the Savoy Hotel on Auburn Avenue.

Margaret Mitchell never wrote another novel.  At the age of 49, **she died after being struck by a taxi** as she attempted to cross Peachtree near 13th Street.  Ironically, she was herself a notoriously bad driver.  Mitchell is buried in Oakland Cemetery, under her married name of Marsh.

**The Road to Tara Museum** is located in the lower level of the Georgian Terrace Hotel, across from the Fox Theatre.  Although the museum is not terribly large, there is a denseness of information and many wonderful photographs are on display.  At the formal entrance to the **Academy of Medicine Building** (875 West Peachtree) hangs a chandelier used in the film.  This 1940 building is a clubhouse for physicians.

A **Gone With the Wind Theme Park** is being planned.  Located in the small town of Villa Rica, west of Atlanta in Douglas County, the park opens in 1995.  Site of the former Flying S Dude Ranch, the theme park promises tasteful and mature depictions of that era in Southern Culture.

# Chapter 10
## The Segregationist Tour

**M**any persons who haven't spent any amount of time in the South harbor preconceived and stereotypical notions about the state of civil rights in the region. In fact, many Northerners refuse to travel south of the Mason-Dixon line; many southerners are reluctant to travel north of it. Those who work up their courage and travel for the first time to the south are often intensely interested in talking with southerners about the "problem" of integration, and in what it means to be a southerner today.

It's a prickly subject. People like to discuss it, especially on talk radio. Everyone has an opinion. We here in the *Sideways Atlanta* home office believe that history is history, and the eras of slavery, segregation, and civil rights activism are some of the most intensely interesting Atlanta has to offer.

Over the last few years, the state of Georgia has been embroiled in a controversy over **the state flag**, which has as two-thirds of its design the old confederate national flag. Some argue the flag simply acknowledges the heritage of the state. Others feel the flag is a white supremecist slap in the face. It was in 1956, 21 months after the supreme court made its school desegregation decision, that the Georgia state legislature voted to change the state flag to include the rebel flag. Governor Marvin Griffin declared, "Georgia will have separate public schools or no public schools." Today, it is generally agreed that the whole issue is problematic, especially since it touched off a slew of similar complaints about other racist practices, including the controversial "tomahawkin" done at the Atlanta Braves baseball games. It seems that disagreement is never far from the surface, no matter what position any individual or group takes.

Atlanta was a city where **slaves were brokered** and moved to farms and plantations all around the region. One broker, Robert A. Crawford, Negro Dealer, located his business at 10 Peachtree Street, now just outside of Underground Atlanta.

Reconstruction days found newly-freed slaves gravitating toward urban areas in hopes of finding new direction in their lives. Churches were among the first to be reorganized as independent bodies. **The First Baptist Church of Atlanta** originally gathered in a railroad box car. The railroads played an important part in Reconstruction as cotton was brought to Atlanta to be shipped elsewhere. It was also a distribution center for goods shipped from the North. The fast growth of the city accommodated a new black business class to serve an expanding black clientele. However, two totally separate cultures were produced, one for blacks and one for whites.

Eighteen ninety-five saw the **Cotton States and International Exposition**, a self-promotional event held in Atlanta. Booker T. Washington, a black educator, gave a speech promoting segregation and self-reliance as a tool for advancement. Only one year later, Federal law adopted segregation as national policy, both in the north and the south.

Problems beginning during Reconstruction continued into the beginning of the next century, culminating in widespread riots both in 1902 and 1906.

**The 1902 shootout** took place in the Pittsburg section of Atlanta which is located, roughly, in the area bordered by railroad tracks on the east, Stewart Avenue on the west, University to the south, and Ralph D. Abernathy to the north. The riot began when a former policeman was attacked by several Negroes. The men retreated to a house, shooting at the policemen who came to arrest them. Four policemen were killed and four wounded. Three Negroes were killed. The house they were holed up in (at Delevan & McDaniel) was burned, along with several other nearby homes, in order to smoke out the desperadoes. The Pittsburg area was besieged by hundreds of curious who converged on the house where the shootout occurred. Onlookers carried off most of the remains of the house as souvenirs. The Governor sent in a regiment of soldiers to restore order, which mostly meant keeping the sightseers under control.

Things hadn't improved much by 1906 when, after a gubernatorial election whose issues centered around ways to assure Negro disfranchisement, riots again broke out. Note both sides of the election agreed that the Negro vote should be disenfranchised; the controversy was simply over the most effective way to accomplish it. In addition, there was a push to separate taxes so white taxes only paid for white school children, and Negro taxes paid for their own children's education.

Amazingly, these issues did not start **the riot of 1906**. It was the unrest created by increasing reports of white women being molested, culminating with four in the same day. Ultimately, the riots were started by a Saturday night crowd of about twenty rowdy and drunken youths worried about the lack of respect paid towards white women by "Negro brutes." It was time to go out and do a bit of "Negro chasing." This all took place around the corner of Pryor and Decatur streets. Before the first altercation ended, only about two hours later, the mob had grown to 2,000. The mob was briefly dispersed by the fire department spraying water on them, but rose up in greater force later, in an attack on a trolley car carrying Negroes. Three men were beaten to death. By this time, the crowd had grown to about 3,000. Chief Joyner, Captain of the Fire Department, was ordered by the mayor to hose the rioters. It did not help the situation. Joyner, also an authority on Brunswick Stew, became mayor a year later. A relief of him is on display outside of **Fire House Number One**, just east of Atlanta University near Markham, Techwood, and Chapel Streets.

Near Marietta and Forsyth streets, two Negro barbers were killed, and soon after, another man was killed on the Forsyth street bridge. The end total of dead was two white and ten Negro, with seventy wounded. Six hundred military personnel were called in to restore order, which consisted mostly of searching for weapons on all Negroes brave enough to be out on the streets.

Surprisingly, there was very little impetus in the Negro community for actions of retaliation. Several meetings were held, but were promptly broken up by the police who arrested the leaders. Once again, temporarily, the streets of Atlanta were safe for white women to walk! The riot did, however, lead to the creation of **Auburn Avenue** as an area for black business, social, and entertainment activity.

**The Ku Klux Klan**, founded in December of 1865 in Pulaski, Tennessee, found a stronghold in the Atlanta area. Scholars at the turn of the century studying the Reconstruction era decided emancipation had been a mistake and promoted the idea of restoring lands to the plantation owners, concluding that Negroes would never achieve civilization or appreciate freedom. Klan activity did subside, eventually. The D.W. Griffith epic of 1915, *Birth of a Nation,* glorified the Klan and visualized the ideas of the scholars. Griffith was surprised and hurt when the NAACP organized a boycott and picketed the cinemas showing the film.

In 1916 the Klan, or the "Invisible Empire," was resurrected in a ceremony on the top of nearby Stone Mountain, and was later given legal rights by the State of Georgia. For many, many years, May 6 saw an annual pilgrimage to Stone Mountain where crosses were burned. The resurrection was also due, in part, to Leo Frank's murder of 13-year-old Mary Phagan in 1913. Frank's Jewish heritage fed the flame of controversy which resulted in him being lynched and hanged in 1915. In 1921, the Klan bought a building at the southeast corner of Peachtree Road and East Wesley Road. As Atlanta was then the national headquarters for the Klan, this building served as the Imperial Palace. The Klan also occupied, at one time, rooms 1118-1122 in the Wynne-Claughton building, downtown in back of the Winecoff Hotel.

The Cotton Exchange Building, at 3155 Roswell in Buckhead, was supposedly where Klan robes were manufactured. It is now occupied by a law firm.

Through the twenties, the Ku Klux Klan is said to have controlled the Atlanta city government. Their influence waned, but picked up again during the 30s depression era, when one of their principal activities was to try to prevent Negroes from voting.

The 1930s saw many attempts to keep segregation the normal order of business. The Ponce de Leon Development Corporation bought up abandoned property along Ponce de Leon Avenue in order to block the path of black migration by creating a sort of **"racial buffer zone"** between black and white.

The hoopla surrounding **the premier of *Gone With the Wind*** in 1939 was clouded by the exclusion of the movie's black actors and actresses from the festivities. Although this slight was protested by the Hollywood contingent, action was not taken for fear of upsetting the joyous (and oblivious) citizens of Atlanta. The main festivities were held at the Georgian Terrace Ballroom on Peachtree and Ponce de Leon; the blacks held their own celebration at the Savoy Hotel on Auburn Ave.

**Desegregation of Atlanta restaurants** began in 1960 with groups organized to target various stores. One was the lunch counter at 180 Peachtree Street, then Davidson's, now Macy's. Most demonstrations were peaceful. Business owners coped by turning off their lights, refusing service, and closing altogether if necessary.

The 1960s were an important and very volatile time for the city of Atlanta. Issues of civil rights made significant gains during this time, over screams of protest and violence. Led by **Dr. Martin Luther King, Jr., headquartered at the Ebenezer Baptist Church on Auburn Avenue**, blacks threatened economic boycott as a push towards desegregation.

**Lester Maddox**, later Governor of Georgia, had his own headquarters during this turbulent time, his **Pickrick Cafe**, located at 891 Hemphill Avenue, right on the outskirts of Georgia Tech. This building is now a student placement center for Georgia Tech. Maddox daily dished up his special Pickrick Meatloaf "with or without opinions." His newspaper ads for the restaurant were an eclectic combination of southern philosophy, politics, and promises of good eating. He never desegregated the Pickrick, choosing to close it down instead. As Governor, Lester Maddox instituted his popular "Little People's Sunday," an open house where anyone could visit him in the Governor's Mansion (then in Ansley Park) to talk about problems and issues. In April 1967, four escaped convicts and one of the convict's mothers showed up at the open house. The convicts described the awful conditions at their prison, and as a result, Maddox ordered a complete investigation of the state's prisons and work camps. The Governor also worked to eliminate clip joints (shell games, dice games) operating along the route Yankees traditionally took to Florida. Maddox was, and is, an unusual man. Now living in Newt Gingrich's Sixth Congressional District, he still makes appearances, occasionally riding his bicycle backwards (a habit begun while courting his wife). Souvenirs of Governor Maddox's political life can still be found in area antique stores. One good place to look for Maddoxabilia is at **Kudzu Antiques**, located on Ponce de Leon in Decatur, about a mile past the Avondale Metro stop.

Atlanta saw many mass demonstrations before and after segregation "officially" ended in 1965 with the passage of the Voting Rights Act. As late as 1966, Atlanta tried to enforce the old anti-insurrection laws, arresting radical leader Stokely Carmichael.

Your segregationist explorations of Atlanta would be woefully incomplete without a cautious visit to **Wildman's Civil War Supply Store** in Kennesaw. This town, located on route 41 north of Atlanta, is notorious for the ordinance that requires each head of household to own a gun. In addition to a very fine collection of Civil War literature, Wildman's is a headquarters for a Civil War re-enactment group. What gives this place a bite, however, is the large collection of Ku Klux Klan memorabilia (not for sale!), including a robed figure looming in the back of the store. The figure stands guard near a locked cabinet containing new (and for sale) white Klan robes. There are books and pamphlets supporting the white supremacist philosophy, plus boxes of free tear sheets, cartoons, and other bits of "evidence." Posters, postcards, photographs, and bumper stickers are also available. Be prepared for surprising displays of racist thought. Leave Wildman's with the understanding that many different philosophies are alive and well in our culture today.

There are other good places to shop for remnants of the segregationist south, if you aren't too embarrassed to actually pay money for them. In addition to the already-mentioned Kudzu Antiques, the whole town of Chamblee is loaded with antique shops and southern memorabilia. Plan on staying the whole day in Chamblee if you want to cover everything.

It is hard to create a logical driving tour of segregationist Atlanta, so we have listed here for you a checklist, and hope you will incorporate some of these places in your other driving expeditions:

   \_\_\_\_\_   **Negro Dealer, 10 Peachtree Street**
   \_\_\_\_\_   **Pittsburgh, scene of 1902 riot**
   \_\_\_\_\_   **Corner of Pryor & Decatur, start of 1906 riots**
   \_\_\_\_\_   **Lunch Counter at 180 Peachtree Street (Macy's)**
   \_\_\_\_\_   **KKK National Headquarters & Imperial Palace, 2621 Peachtree Street**
   \_\_\_\_\_   **KKK robe factory, 3155 Roswell Road**
   \_\_\_\_\_   **Ponce de Leon "buffer zone"**
   \_\_\_\_\_   **Georgian Ballroom (Peachtree and Ponce) and the Savoy Hotel on Auburn Avenue**
   \_\_\_\_\_   **Ebenezer Baptist Church, Civil Rights Headquarters on Auburn Avenue**
   \_\_\_\_\_   **Pickrick Cafe, 891 Hemphill Avenue**
   \_\_\_\_\_   **Top of Stone Mountain**
   \_\_\_\_\_   **Wildman's, Kennesaw, Georgia**
   \_\_\_\_\_   **Kudzu Antiques, Decatur, Georgia**
   \_\_\_\_\_   **Chamblee, Georgia (many antique stores)**

**Wildman's**

**The Pickrick Cafe**

**Lunch Counter at Macy's (formerly Davidson's)**

# Chapter 11
## A Civil Rights Tour

**W**e begin our Civil Rights tour in the **Vine City** section of Atlanta, an area important in the development of black cultural pride and civil rights strategies.

First stop is the home of **Alonzo Herndon**, a man who began life as a slave and ended it as one of America's wealthiest black businessmen. The Herndon Home is located at 587 University Place, NW, west of the center of town on Martin Luther King, Jr. Drive (MLK). Call 581-9813 for hours; admission is free. The mansion, built in 1910, was designed by Herndon himself. Built by black labor, the fifteen room home is an example of the Classical Beaux Arts style.

Continue west along MLK to Ashby. Along the way, you will pass **Morris Brown College** on your right, and **Atlanta University** on your left. Morris Brown, established in 1881, was the first college in Georgia founded by blacks. Atlanta University was originally founded by white missionaries in 1867. Stop at the **Paschal Motor Hotel and Restaurant** at 830 MLK. This was the scene of early civil rights strategies. The restaurant is open daily 7:30 a.m. to 11 p.m.

Turn left on Ashby and head south to Ralph D. Abernathy Avenue (RDA), where you can choose to turn left or right. Go right and head for the **Hammond House**, 503 Peeples, a museum of African-American and Haitian Art. Heading left on RDA Avenue takes you past the **Soul Vegetarian Restaurant** (879). **The Shrine of the Black Madonna Culture Center**, at 946 (752-6125) also houses an African-American bookstore, said to be the largest in the country.

Continue heading east on Ralph D. Abernathy. Head north on Central, which will take you through the downtown/5 Points area. Look toward your left when you cross Decatur to see where the **1906 race riots** started (Decatur & Pryor is two blocks to your left; Marietta & Forsyth is six blocks to your left). Both sites, located in the heart of 5

Points, are best seen on the walking tour of the downtown area.

As you turn right off Central onto Auburn, you are entering a densely rich area of civil rights history and African-American culture. **Auburn Avenue's** first settler was Hardy Ivy. His tract of land covered most of what is now Auburn. In 1856, Mary Combs became the first black property owner in Atlanta when she bought land at Peachtree & Auburn (then known as Wheat Street). She later sold her land to buy freedom for her husband. You might want to make your first stop on Auburn the **APEX Museum** (135) for an introduction to African heritage and the "Sweet Auburn" experience. Call 521-2654 for hours.

Continue east on Auburn. You will pass many historically significant landmarks, but take special note of the **Royal Peacock Club** (184-86), built in 1922. Originally named the Top Hat, this was Atlanta's first black nightclub (reserved for whites Saturday nights only). Although many local musicians dominated the club, it played host to giants such as B.B. King. The club continued as a music center into the 50s and 60s; Jimi Hendrix supposedly met Little Richard here.

At Butler Street, note the **Big Bethel African Methodist Episcopal Church**, in 1868 becoming the first black church on Auburn. Go right on Butler to see the **Butler Street YMCA**, another place where activists plotted the Civil Rights movement. **The Atlanta Municipal Market**, one block further down, at Edgewood, is a very large market offering fresh fruits, vegetables, and meats.

Back on Auburn, see the **Herndon Building** at 231-45. Herndon, who started his empire with a barbershop at 66 Peachtree Street (known as the Crystal Palace), expanded his business interests and his wealth by founding the Atlanta Life Insurance Company.

Pass under the Interstates 75/85, and at the NW corner of Hilliard, note the **Prince Hall Masonic Building**, national headquarters of the Southern Christian Leadership Conference (SCLC). Formerly headed by Dr. Martin Luther King, Jr., this organization was an important catalyst in the fight for civil rights.

Founded in 1870, the **Wheat Street Baptist Church** (365) will be on your right. Before entering the National Park Service area (**the Martin Luther King, Jr. National Historical Site**), you might want to stop for a bite to eat at the **Beautiful Restaurant**, located at the corner of Jackson Street, next door to the **Ebenezer Baptist Church**. Looking north up Jackson you can see the area where author Margaret Mitchell spent her early childhood years.

When you are ready to enter the National Park complex, we recommend you park and head on foot for the information kiosk, located one-half block on your left. Here you can orient yourself to this very dense area: allow several hours for this section alone. Be sure to see the Ebenezer Baptist Church where Martin Luther King, Jr. served as co-pastor with his father, Martin Luther King, Sr. (also known as Daddy King). The Center for Non-Violent Social Change houses a small exhibit, King's grave lit by an eternal flame, and is the starting point for a good walking tour of King's birth home and the neighborhood he grew up in. Other tours begin at the Bryant-Graves House (522 Auburn, east of the birth home). Bookstores are located both at the Bryant-Graves house and at the Freedom Hall Complex.

Some of Reverend King's right-hand men are still working to preserve his ideals and advance the Civil Rights cause. The Reverend Jesse Jackson, an outspoken national leader, may yet be President of the United States. Longtime Atlanta mayor Andrew Young coined the anagram **SAWBS** (pronounced "sobs") to describe Smart Ass White Boys, especially ones who disagreed with him. We like that! We're not so crazy about his penchant for tearing down old Atlanta and replacing it with glassy office buildings. City Councilman Hosea Williams is still a very controversial figure on the Atlanta scene.

King was originally buried at **Southview Cemetery**. His parents, Daddy King and Alberta Williams King, are buried there still. You can get to Southview by heading south on Boulevard (turn right off Auburn after the Freedom Hall Complex). Right after you go under the railroad tracks, you will see Cabbagetown on your left. On your right you will pass the lovely Oakland Cemetery; Grant Park, featuring Zoo Atlanta and the Cyclorama will also be on your right. When Boulevard ends at the Federal Penitentiary, go right on McDonough, left on Sawtell, and right on Jonesboro Road (route 54). Southview will be on your left. Also buried here are some of the victims of the 1902 Pittsburg shootout, and many ex-slaves.

Return to town by heading back northwest on Jonesboro which joins McDonough, takes a hard left, and connects to the 75/85 interstate south of the city.

# Hosea Williams
## An Atlanta Treasure

Hosea Williams, "Atlanta's Most Notorious Driver," drives a 1984 blue Cadillac. Watch out for him! He has had over 30 traffic charges since 1967, but claims they are all part of a police conspiracy to harass him. Why?

Reverend Hosea Williams was one of the Reverend Martin Luther King, Jr.'s right-hand men. He was with King on the day King was assassinated in Memphis. He was the director of the Southern Christian Leadership Conference from 1969-71, served as a State Legislator, Atlanta City Councilman, DeKalb County Commissioner, and advisor to then-President Ronald Reagan.

A man with 128 career arrests, Williams led a "Walk for Brotherhood" march in Forsyth County (Cumming, Georgia) in 1987, to protest the lack of a black presence in the area. The 90 marchers were met by about 400 anti-brotherhood protesters, including representatives from the Ku Klux Klan and former Governor Lester Maddox. The event turned violent, creating national publicity. A countermarch was planned for the next week. Although the anti-brotherhood protesters were ready, led by former Klan leader David Duke, they were not prepared for the 20,000 marchers that descended on the town, led by the Reverend Williams. Marchers this time included Coretta Scott King, Benjamin Hooks, RuPaul, and the Guardian Angels.

Today, Williams runs a Bingo Parlor, and in 1995 celebrated his 25th annual "Feed the Hungry Christmas Dinner." He is host of the weekly cable TV talk show, "The Voice of the Crusader." Hosea Williams believes the modern Civil Rights movement has sold out and that it no longer works to achieve the dream of Martin Luther King, Jr. He is one of Atlanta's great living treasures. His motto was, and remains, "Unbossed and Unbought."

# Chapter 12
# Murder and Mayhem

**I**n 1861 one "good" citizen of Atlanta was murdered. Who knows how many "bad" citizens met untimely ends that year; history records just one "good" one. Dead after a beating by two brothers, John and James Wilson, was **Thomas Terry**, owner of a sawmill on Sugar Creek, near the future site of the Battle of Atlanta. It was an ironic twist of fate that freed the convicted James Wilson. When Sherman began his march through Georgia, Wilson was freed with all the other prisoners in a desperate attempt to draft more men in the fight for the Confederacy.

**The first recorded murder** took place in 1848. A man named McWilliams was stabbed to death by Bill Terrell, who escaped capture.

July 26, 1879 saw the double murder of **Martin and Susan DeFoor**. While asleep in their home, the elderly pair were almost decapitated by an ax. There was no apparent motive as no money or property was taken, nor did the DeFoors have any known enemies. Evidence of watermelon seeds in a pile of excrement led authorities to believe the murderer was a Negro, but despite many arrests, the murders were never solved. Martin DeFoor was one of the first settlers in the Fort Peachtree area, taking over Montgomery's Ferry and renaming it DeFoor's Ferry. DeFoor and his wife are buried in the Montgomery Family Cemetery. The DeFoor house was located on the road to Iceville (Bolton Road), north of Moore's Mill Road on Chattahoochee Avenue.

A car accident in 1904 was recorded in great detail, as it was the first vehicular death in Atlanta. **Mr. and Mrs. Frank Reynolds**, with two companions, flipped their car, a White Steamer, at the bottom of the hill about one mile southeast of Bolton Road and Marietta Boulevard, on Marietta. Frank Reynolds died at the scene; Addie Reynolds died later, despite (or perhaps because of) several injections of strychnine and whiskey.  One of the passengers, a Miss Elmer George, was lauded for her bravery despite a sprained ankle, bruised head, and a severely shocked nervous system.  Miss George, in a surge of strength, lifted the car off the body of another passenger and revived him so he could go to the assistance of the Reynolds couple.

Many murders in and around Atlanta have never been solved.  Between 1911 and 1912, one murderer, named **"Jack the Ripper"** by the Atlanta press, preyed exclusively on Negro women of mixed blood, killing twenty in all.  Each woman was found strangled, and with her throat slit.  "Carved" was the word used to describe mutilations on other parts of their bodies.  Coincidentally, during those same years, more than 40 ax murders of similar women in Texas and Louisiana also went unsolved.  Please note the real "Jack the Ripper" in London only killed six!

Another notorious murder, also with a racial bias, took place in 1913 at the National Pencil Company (39 S. Forsyth Street near Alabama, just south of Underground).  A fourteen-year-old girl, **Mary Phagan**, who worked at the factory, stopped by on Saturday, April 26 (also Confederate Memorial Day) to collect her pay of one dollar and twenty cents for the week.  Her body was discovered in the factory basement the next morning.  Mary had been beaten and strangled.  Two notes, written in crude Negro dialect, were found near the body.  Implicated first was the night watchman, and later, a janitor, but eventually the Jewish supervisor of the plant, Leo M. Frank, was indicted.  During the trial, spectators packed picnic lunches so they could enjoy the spectacle without having to get up (and relinquish their seats).  Vendors also sold sandwiches and mince pies during the trial, which lasted twenty-nine days.

Frank, after making a four hour statement on his own behalf, was found guilty and sentenced to be hanged.  Although appealed on the grounds that public opinion against Frank swayed the verdict, prosecuters argued against a retrial, citing mob action as a problem.  The National Guard was put on alert.

Controversy continued into 1915, with most opinions running against Frank.  Several stays of execution and a commuted sentence incited mobs to attack the Governor's mansion and a fellow convict to slash Frank's throat.  The final events came on August 16, 1915, when twenty-five men staged a raid on the prison at Milledgeville, cutting wires, disarming the guards, and abducting Leo Frank.  The next morning his body, with a white handkerchief placed over his face, was found hanging from a tree along the Marietta-Roswell Road. Two photographs were taken, and later made into postcards. One of the photographs can be seen at Wild Bill's Cherokee Barbershop on Tenth Street near Howell Mill Road. A judge arriving on the scene prevented Frank's body from being divided up into souvenirs. The body was on view to the thousands who came to the funeral parlor at Houston and Ivy. It was later shipped to Brooklyn for burial at Mt. Carmel Cemetery. Little Mary Phagan is buried in the Citizen's Cemetery at Marietta. The twenty-five men who raided the prison were never identified.

Frank B. DuPre reigned as the **"Peachtree Bandit"** in 1922. DuPre was described as a beady-eyed ex-sailor, with a way with the ladies. During the Christmas shopping season of 1921, where Underground Atlanta is now, DuPre, while stealing a diamond ring for his girlfriend Betty Andrews, shot and killed Irby C. Walker, a Pinkerton man. Fleeing into the Kimball House Hotel, where he had rooms and where Betty was waiting, he shot another man and continued his escape, terrorizing thousands of Christmas shoppers. Police found a gray overcoat, touching off a manhunt of such proportions that one headline read, "Owners of Gray Overcoats Safer by Own Fireside."

DuPre escaped by taxi and was dropped off in Chattanooga, Tennessee. The discovery of the diamond ring at a pawnshop in Chattanooga was quickly followed by the discovery of Betty. On January 13, DuPre was recognized in Detroit by two detectives, one of whom told him, "I'll blow you back to Atlanta if you move!"

Back in Atlanta, DuPre was lauded as a romantic figure by groups of women who prayed and sang in the rain, right up till his death by hanging. Thousands turned out for the event. Children cried, "Goodbye, Frank, goodbye. Be brave!" Frank's last words were to Betty, who was standing on the balcony of a nearby building. "Betty, listen," he cried. "You're going to meet me in heaven, ain't you?" Frank B. DuPre was the last person to be hanged in Georgia. It was said his ghost lurked for years around the Fulton Tower (the Atlanta Jail, near Georgia State).

Escapees of the Federal Penitentiary in southeast Atlanta terrorized residents of the Lakewood Heights area in March of 1923 when they kidnapped a man who then refused to drive them into the country. **Gerald Chapman**, in jail for a $3 million mail heist, and **Frank Grey**, a forger, overpowered a nurse, tied sheets together, and lowered themselves out of a second floor window. When Mr. W.H. Edwards refused to help them, he was used as a hostage so they could board a streetcar and make their getaway. They then enlisted the aid of a taxi driver, who drove them to Athens, where they were eventually captured by a posse of citizens who found them hiding in a cotton patch.

**Richard Gray Gallogly and George Harsh,** students and fraternity brothers at Oglethorpe University, teamed up in 1928 to collaborate on a series of holdups which culminated in two murders. One robbery took place at the Atlantic and Pacific Tea Store at 1004 Hemphill Avenue. The other was at the 8th Street Pharmacy at 908 Boulevard (now the Sig Samuels Dry Cleaning on Monroe). The men were tied to the murders using a new technique of comparing empty shell casings from each murder with the guns owned by the young men. Harsh was traced through a pair of trousers bloodied after one of the holdups. Harsh claimed the "whiskey made me do it" defense. Gallogly was captured while celebrating after a University of Georgia football victory over Tulane.

Both boys were members of socially prominent families. They were each sentenced to life in prison. Connections were made between their case and that of Leopold and Loeb, in Chicago. Both sets of young men killed just for the thrill of it.

Willard Smith, one of the victims, is buried at West View Cemetery. Samuel Meek, the other victim, lies in the Powder Springs Cemetery.

In 1939, Gallogly escaped while being transfered from an Atlanta hospital to a prison in Reidsville. His wife of four months was with him; she presumably supplied the gun he used. Gallogly's mother also accompanied the group, but she refused to go with her son and walked back to town with the guards. He was eventually recaptured.

Harsh spent twelve years on a Georgia chain gang, and was pardoned after saving the life of a fellow prisoner. He joined the Royal Canadian Air Force, fought against the Germans in World War II, was captured, and sent to the Stalag III prison camp, taking part in the infamous "Great Escape" story. Harsh died in Toronto in 1980 at the age of 82.

**Traveling salesman Max Sjoblom** was killed and dumped near Flat Rock Church in Clayton County. Sjoblom was the victim of a 1934 carjacking at Marietta and Spring Streets. Robert Riley and his friend Hoyt Summers were working on their third such robbery of the evening on September 22,

1934. And although many people saw Riley and Summers heading back to Atlanta from where they tossed the body, it was fifteen hours before anyone made any connections. After the men were arrested, Riley led police out to Sjoblom's body. Summers maintained his innocence, but a torn dollar bill found both on Summers and on Sjoblom left no doubts.

On April 26, 1935, twenty-two years to the day after the murder of little Mary Phagan, another gruesome killing occurred. **Jimmie Rosenfield**, of Brooklyn, NY, a member of the Dutch Schultz gang there, had come to Atlanta to lay low for awhile. Once in town, he realized he had a whole new territory at his disposal and organized various gambling, burglary, and robbery activities. He got involved with Mrs. R.B. (Frances) Bullock, and on Confederate Memorial Day, in a classic case of mistaken identity, shot and killed Lester Stone, neighbor of the Bullocks. This all happened at the apartment building at 572 Parkway Drive. The Bullocks, afraid Rosenfield would shoot them too, pretended to know nothing of why their friend was shot in front of their door. It wasn't until when a routine investigation of another burglary turned up new evidence that a break in the case was made. Although Rosenfield received a life sentence for the murder of Lester Stone (the Bullocks were arrested but not charged), his sentence was commuted by the Governor and he returned immediately to Brooklyn.

Nineteen forty-three brought tragedy to Druid Hills. **Henry C. Heinz**, a socially prominent civic leader, was murdered by a masked man in the library of his home at 1610 Ponce de Leon Avenue. It was thought that, because of the mask, Heinz might have known his assailant, who turned out to be Horace Blalock, a Negro railroad worker and habitual burglar. Blalock led police to the spot on the middle of the Bolton bridge over the Chattahoochee River (at Standing Peachtree) where he had thrown the gun and other possessions of Heinz. Blalock's case was the first to use fingerprint technology. He was paroled in 1955 and moved to Vidalia. Henry C. Heinz is buried in West View Cemetery, but his ghost supposedly haunts the grounds of his old home (now the Lullwater Estates).

In another murder seething with intrique, the body of **Mrs. Paul Refoule** was discovered in Peachtree Creek in back of her home at 2450 Howell Mill Road. She was found on May 15, 1947 strangled, her feet tied together. Mr. Refoule was an art instructor at the High Museum of Art. Peggy Refoule was also an artist, having studied at the Sorbonne, where she met her husband. Paul Refoule, the #1 suspect right from the beginning, confessed to "unnatural sex practices" with a female art student. In those days, sodomy alone carried with it a life imprisonment sentence. Refoule, who had been considering divorce, also failed a lie detector test, but was never charged with the crime. He died of lung cancer the next year.

Another unsolved murder dating from just six weeks before the Refoule murder was the killing of **Mrs. Jeanette Reyman** of Bogart. Both Refoule and Reyman were mothers in their early thirties; they were both slain on a Wednesday afternoon. Both had been assaulted, both had part of their underwear missing, and both women's feet were bound together. Reyman was last seen shopping at the Sears Building on Ponce. Her body was found in a truck parked on Moreland, near Flat Shoals Avenue.

Atlanta murders went national in 1949, when, on April 21, **John Garris**, tenor of the Metropolitan Opera, was found in an alley off Thurmond Street. He had been shot once in the heart. Grover Pulley, an ex-con, was later arrested with a gun "similar" to the one used to kill Garris. The case was thrown out for lack of evidence, and the murder remains unsolved.

**Nub Norton**, a one-armed parking lot attendant with a long history of robbery and larceny, was found shot three times in the Little Five Points area off Edgewood Avenue on October 20, 1954. Within two days, it was learned he had been riding around town with two men busy committing their own string of robberies. Earnest Bishop and Roy Lee Carroll had carried out three robberies, two at the same Viaduct Package Store at 647 Edgewood Avenue. Norton joined up with them, but got into an argument with Bishop, who shot his old friend and dumped the body. Afterwards, Bishop and Carroll had a few beers, registered at a nearby hotel, hit a few other establishments (and a woman on the head), before being picked up by the police at Bell near Decatur St.

In 1964 a young Atlanta housewife, pregnant again, shot and killed her husband, three children, and herself. **The Richardson Family** of 1284 Woodland Avenue is buried together in Decatur Cemetery. Before the murders, Mrs. Richardson told a neighbor, perhaps over coffee at the nearby Dunk n' Dine, "If I'm pregnant again, I'm going to kill myself."

On April 17, 1964, **three Gwinnet County policemen** were handcuffed, lined up, and shot in the head with their own guns on lonely Arc Road near Lawrenceville. Fourteen months later, a confession was extracted from one of the murderers. The murders occurred while three men, including a former Gwinnet County sheriff, were stripping a stolen car when the three policemen showed up unexpectedly.

Citizens of the entire United States focused their attention on Atlanta on December 17, 1968, when an Emory University coed, the daughter of a wealthy Florida family, was abducted from the Rodeway Inn on Clairmont Road, where she was visiting with her mother. **Barbara Jane Mackle**, age 20, was kidnapped by a man pretending to be a cop. Barbara Jane was then buried alive in a box which also contained food, water, a fan, and an air pump. She was buried about 18 inches down off the Berkeley Lake Road near the Peachtree Industrial Highway, in the woods. The kidnappers, after receiving a $500,000 ransom, released her location. She was freed after spending 80 hours in the box. Gary S. Krist and his companion, Ruth Eisenman Schien, a Honduran, were charged with the crime and convicted. Ruth spent seven years in Milledgeville, and was then deported. Krist, sentenced to life imprisonment in Reidsville, was paroled after ten years on the condition he never return to Georgia. Krist married and moved to Sitka, Alaska, his boyhood home. As soon as his probation ran out, he returned to Georgia to visit relatives.

A particularly heartbreaking tragedy occurred Sunday, June 30, 1974, when the mother of slain civil rights leader Martin Luther King, Jr. was also assassinated while she played the "Lord's Prayer" on the organ at the Ebenezer Baptist Church. The gunman, Marcus Wayne Chenault, 21, of Dayton, Ohio, had been ordered by God to kill the Reverend Martin Luther "Daddy" King, Sr. One other man was also killed that day, and two others were injured. **Mrs. Alberta W. King, Sr.** was not the immediate target of the gunman, an education major at Ohio State University. Chenault had a list of civil rights leaders, including the Reverend Ralph David Abernathy and the Reverend Jesse Jackson, who were targeted for death.

When "Daddy" King asked Chenault why he had shot his wife, the gunman replied, "Because she was a Christian, and all Christians are my enemies."

**Paul John Knowles** was a habitual killer, thought to have slain at least 25 people during the course of 1974. His killing spree ranged from his home state of Florida, into Georgia, and perhaps on to Ohio and Connecticut. Ms. Sandy Fawkes, a British journalist, spent two days and nights in the Holiday Inn of downtown Atlanta with an impotent man who turned out to be Knowles.  In her book, "Killing Time," Fawkes describes, in language more appropriate to a romance novel, her encounter with a Lincolnesque man with a strong jawline who claimed to be a businessman from New Mexico.  She met him in the bar of the hotel and he got her into bed the same evening.  Next morning, she learned his name, "Lester Daryl Golden."  They spent the day wandering around Atlanta, exploring and shopping in Peachtree Center.  While spending some quiet time drinking Planter's Punch at the Hyatt Regency Hotel's revolving Polaris restaurant and lounge, Knowles asked the journalist to write a book about him.  He said he hadn't long to live.

Paul John Knowles was shot to death a month after his capture while he was supposedly showing officers where he had tossed a gun.  The policemen alleged Knowles got loose from his handcuffs and tried to grab a gun.  They shot him in self-defense.  The car, traveling on Route 20 west of Atlanta, went off the road about 100 yards east of Lee Road (Douglas County).

"Ain't nobody shedding no tears down here," a Florida cop was reputed to say.

Nineteen seventy-seven was a very bad year for lovers in Atlanta.  In three separate incidents, each occuring approximately four weeks apart, a lone gunman, dubbed the **"Lover's Lane Killer,"** shot into cars of young lovers parked in various lover's lanes in southwest Atlanta.  The first shooting took place on January 16 in Adams Park, when two persons were found shot to death in their car.  Twenty-seven days later, he struck in West Manor Park, shooting both occupants who miraculously survived.  They described a large black man who knelt and shot like a policeman would.  Twenty-eight days later, two more lovers were shot, again in Adams Park.  One died.  The hunt for the killer tightened up when police perceived the 4-week pattern, and set up an elaborate and secret stakeout during the weekend of April 4 to 6.  The killer did not show up, and has not been heard from since.  Police blamed the media for leaking the story after the failed stakeout, and only then began warning young lovers to stay out of the parks after dark.

As part of their investigation, police officers held a private screening of the film *The Town That Dreaded Sundown* (1977), about a similar case of lover's lane killings in Texarkana.

**In 1979, Atlanta was named as America's Murder Capital.**

Probably the most notorious of all Atlanta murders were the mysterious killings of twenty-eight young blacks in the city over a period of two years. At one point, cruel rumors flew over the nation that blacks were killing their own children in order to cast suspicion on the Klan.

In June of 1981, police finally questioned a suspect, 23-year-old **Wayne B. Williams** of 1817 Penelope Drive. Williams had been spotted, in the early hours of May 22, throwing something off the Chattahoochee Bridge (route 280, the James Jackson Parkway). He said it was garbage. Authorities said it was the body of Nathaniel Cater.

Williams, described by friends as a radio and electronic genius, also worked as a freelance television photographer. He drove a van outfitted with all kinds of electronic gadgets and spent his time traveling around the metro area.

Sentenced to life for murdering two young men (but for none of the children), Williams still maintains his innocence. He is serving his term at the prison in Jackson, Georgia. The (unsolved) murders did continue after his arrest, but the media dropped the issue. At various times, mothers of the victims have tried to have the cases reopened.

Urban legend has it that a local disc jockey was fired from his job for playing Queen's "Another One Bites the Dust" after each new body was found.

Nineteen eighty-five and eighty-six saw six killings of young male hustlers by **"Big Mike" Terry,** who alleged self-defense. Terry claimed the smaller men tried to rob him after sex, but received a sentence of life in prison without parole. And, just in case he manages to get out early, four other cases are being held in reserve!

In January of 1990, **Marvin Yizar**, a private detective, shot and set fire to his landlord. Yizar, a Mayoral candidate who lost to Andrew Young in 1985, also ran for City Council in 1986, burning the campaign headquarters of his opponent, P. Martin Cook. Yizar's landlord, real estate broker Julius Iteld, came to the Atlanta Investigations, Inc. at 181 10th Street (between Piedmont and Juniper) to collect $5,700 in back rent. Yizar shot Iteld there, and took the body to a field in Norcross, where he burned it to conceal its identity. Iteld was identified by his wedding ring, and Yizar got life in prison.

**The Perimeter Mall Murderer** let loose on April 24, 1990. James Calvin Brady, recently released from a mental institution, entered the Food Court at the Perimeter Mall at Interstate 285 and the Ashford-Dunwoody Road and opened fire. Standing at the Taco Bell, he aimed toward the Chick-

Fil-A and shot five people, killing one. Turning away, he disposed of the spent shells. Before he could reload, an elderly man approached him, said a few words, and disappeared. Brady threw his gun in a garbage can and left the mall. As the police screeched into the parking lot, he raised up his hands and said, "I'm the one you're looking for." Neighbors told police he had claimed to be possessed by a machine put in his brain and operated by two people from California.

In 1991 **a wrong-way driver** on Interstate 75 drunkenly drove his pick-up truck more than ten miles through rush hour traffic before finally crashing into a family on their way to Disney World. In his wake, Clinton Leigh Hunter, age 33, left nine wrecks. He got on the road at Northside Drive, heading north in the southbound lanes, wreaking havoc past the I-75 and I-285 intersection, finally hitting the family of four near Delk Road, killing the husband. From nearby Marietta, they had just entered the interstate to start their vacation.

Be sure to visit the many murder and mayhem spots identified here as you tour the other interesting facets of life and culture in Atlanta!

Where the Wrong-Way Driver Went Wrong

Bridge across the Chattahoochee River from where
the body of Nathaniel Cater was thrown

Site of one of the Gallogly and Harsh holdups

# Black Week

It may actually be a comfort to those of us who live in the 90s with the daily barrage of death and violence, insanity and crooked deals, that Atlanta actually had a month of violence so profoundly affecting its residents they named the month "Black Week," and recorded the events as a grim aberration of an otherwise gracious culture.

Black Week began in January of 1893 with unseasonably cold temperatures and eight inches of snow. Historians point to the weather as instigator of a horrifying season of suicides, murders, and one bank failure. On January 24, a married man named Umberto Piantini carried out a suicide pact with his girlfriend Selita Muegge at the Metropolitan Hotel (Pryor & Alabama) with gunshot blasts to both their heads. Although Selita survived, the incident seemed to touch off a string of other gruesome events.

On February 19, Aaron Raphael, tired of life, took his own. On February 22, the Gate City National Bank failed. On the 23rd, Tom Cobb Jackson, a young lawyer suffering the stress of everyday life, shot himself in his buggy. On the 24th, a traveling salesman, W.D. Crowley, killed himself over unrequited love.

It was on February 25, however, that Black Week came to its stunning climax. Miss Julia Force, age 34, walked into the rooms of her two sisters and shot each of them in the head. Killed were Florence and Minnie Force. Julia was convinced that her sisters and mother were her enemies. She immediately turned herself in to the police, and was eventually committed to the State Insane Asylum in Millegeville.

The Atlanta Press, near hysteria over this unexplained barrage of murder and suicide, sought to understand the meaning of Julia Force's actions. The papers were filled with accounts of the trial, testimony from family and friends, and finally, with a transcript from Julia's own journals. The article, entitled "RAVINGS-Of a Woman's Maddened Brain," describes circumstances of Julia's birth, as told to her by her mammy.

"Two or three months before I was born," writes Julia, "Mother developed an unsatiable appetite for the coarsest food condiments to an East India degree of fiery seasoning. I was born an apparently healthy child."   (Later)

"When I was about ten weeks old, my body became spotted into boils, which breaking instead of healing spread into discharging sores covering my entire person except my face."

Julia goes on to speculate that these and other health problems, including an inflammation of her eyes which prevented her lashes from growing, stemmed from the spicy food her mother ate while pregnant. Complaints of her mother's insensitive treatment of these afflictions led to the hatred of her mother and of the sisters who collaborated with their mother to perpetuate the agony.

The staff at *Sideways Atlanta* wonders if the "Curry Defense" has ever been promoted before or after to justify aberrant, inexplicable behavior.

Julia Force spent the rest of her life in the State Insane Asylum, and now lies buried, along with the rest of her family, in unmarked graves in the Oakland Cemetery.

Couple overlooking Atlanta, Crest Lawn Cemetery

Pet Heaven

# Chapter 13
# Atlanta's Permanent Residents

**W**e love cemeteries and are especially drawn to old over-grown ones infested with kudzu and/or snakes. Many of Atlanta's are interesting, from the ornate gothic Oakland Cemetery to tiny family plots now surrounded by industry and commerce.

Our favorite cemetery is the old **Montgomery family plot** located near Standing Peachtree. Colonel James Montgomery, founder of Montgomery's Ferry, Indian agent, and first Senator from DeKalb, is buried there with his family. Members of the DeFoor family are also resting there, including Martin and Susan DeFoor, who took over the ferry, renaming it DeFoor's Ferry. They were decapitated while sleeping, becoming Atlanta's first unsolved murder cases. Several unrelated persons and a number of unmarked graves (possibly of slaves) also occupy this heavily overgrown and untended hilltop. The Montgomery Family cemetery is located near the corner of Moore's Mill and Bolton Roads. If driving down Moore's Mill (from a visit to Standing Peachtree), go straight through the parking lot, cross Boulevard, and look for a pharmacy straight ahead. Just to the left, the cemetery is hidden in the brush at the top of a knoll.

Atlanta's first cemetery was located where the Capital City Club (7 Harris at Peachtree) is now. Residents there were eventually moved to Oakland. **Oakland Cemetery**, established in 1850, is also Atlanta's first public park. On the National Register of Historic Places, this victorian-style park offers splendid examples of ornate mausoleums, statuary, and sentiment. All classes of people rest here, including Tweet, a mockingbird, and a dog buried with its owner. Controversy erupted in 1920, when the Boyd family insisted on burying their black maid, Georgia Harris, in the family plot. The

Boyds prevailed, and the maid's remains remain.

An entire afternoon could be consumed just wandering the grounds and admiring the amazing artistry. The cemetery is very densely packed! If time is a factor, it would be wise to join one of the group tours held every Sunday morning at eleven. Oakland provides a map labelled with locations of the graves of many of Atlanta's most well-known residents such as golfer Bobby Jones and author Margaret Mitchell. Large areas were set aside for Confederates, Jews, and Paupers. The Jewish section is especially dense and rich in visual stimulation. Oakland is a place where the architecture competes fiercely for the most beautiful and ornate, at times overwhelming the visitor.

Sideways Atlanta adds a few more spots to look for during your visit to Oakland:

Michael Kenny, who was killed in a jousting tournament at the first Georgia State Fair in Oglethorpe Park, is also here. Dan Lynch, who in 1871 became the city's first firefighter to die in action (he was run over by the fire truck), is buried here.

Jasper N. Smith ("The House That Jack Built"), had a statue of himself made sitting down in front of his mausoleum, without collar or tie, as was his habit in real life. When a vine grew around his neck anyway, he had it cut off. Jack's mausoleum is just to the right as you enter Oakland. The house he built downtown next to the Winekoff Hotel is no longer standing, but the two stone tablets once decorating the house are on display outside the Peachtree MARTA station.

Dr. Albert Hape is best known for bringing ballooning to Atlanta in 1869. Some onlookers wondered if the KKK had a new, scarier means of travel; others wondered if the world was about to end. As they watched, the balloon exploded, but Dr. Hape grabbed a piece of canvas and parachuted to safety. Eventually he came to rest at Oakland.

We always visit the first resident Dr. James Nissen, who had his throat slit before burial, Julia Carlisle Withers (Atlanta's first baby), and the Andrews Raiders plaque on the south wall.

Our favorite place is the unmarked family plot of Julia Force and the two sisters she murdered in 1893. Originator of the "Curry Defense," Julia cleverly surmised that the Indian food her mother ate while pregnant caused her, at the age of 34, to kill Minnie and Florence Force. Unfortunately, the jury didn't agree and declared her insane. Nine members of the family, including Julia and her two sisters, are buried in block 250 (northeast corner), along the west wall of Oakland.

Oakland Cemetery is located just south of the Martin Luther King, Jr. Memorial on Auburn Avenue (turn right on Boulevard and go under the railroad tracks). The Fulton Bag & Cotton Mill will be on your left with Oakland on the right. Turn right on Memorial Drive, and right again to the entrance.

**Westview Cemetery** is located on the site of the Confederate Battle of Ezra Church, on the west side of town off Ralph D. Abernathy Boulevard (route 139). Travel west on I-20 and take exit 17. Westview was the second Atlanta cemetery, established in 1884. It is closed on Saturdays and Sundays.

Check out the three story mausoleum, containing over 11,000 crypts. Marble floors, stained glass, and Mr. Asa Candler's safari trophy room are featured in this massive structure. Unfortunately, the trophy room is not open to the public, and it is not known if any of the many African animal heads remain in the room.

Buried on the rest of Westview's nearly 600 acres are Joel Chandler Harris (the Wren's Nest), Mr. W. Frank Winecoff (the Winecoff Hotel and fire), Laurent DeGive (DeGive's Opera House), Margaret Nichols (a former Miss Atlanta who also died in the Winecoff fire), Charner Humphries of the White Hall Tavern, and many leading men of Atlanta such as Asa G. Candler and Henry W. Grady.

Colonel L.P. Grant (Grant Park) is buried in a plot with his first wife, his second wife, and his second wife's first husband.

Murder victims Peggy Refoule, Henry Heinz, and Willard Smith are all here.

An old Civil War bunker, still intact, is in the back of the cemetery. On the faded tombstone in front of it is carved a Confederate flag.

**Southview Cemetery** was opened in 1886, two years after Westview, on Jonesboro Road (route 54) east of Lakewood Park and south of the Federal Penitentiary. Southview has a large and extremely interesting area devoted to former slaves, and was the original resting place of the Reverend Martin Luther King, Jr. Dr. King's parents are still there. Daddy King's marker reads, "Still in business, just moved upstairs." The victims of the 1902 Pittsburg riot are here.

**Greenwood Cemetery**, established in 1904, is located south of Westview between Cascade and Beecher Roads. A memorial dedicated to the "Hitlerian Holocaust" was erected in 1965 and is in itself worth the visit. Greenwood has a large Jewish population. Rocks placed on graves show someone has visited. Prayer books, which may not be thrown in the trash, also have plots. A mysterious small brick structure turned out to be a prayer book crematorium.

Greenwood has a Chinese section surrounding a 30-foot obelisk, a Greek section complete with a tiny Parthenon, and a Workman's Circle with Arch. Look for a very disturbing baby stone from 1913!

**Hollywood Cemetery**, neatly bisected by Hollywood Road, is reached by traveling west on Bankhead Highway (route 8), and bearing right on Hollywood where the road forks. Many of Atlanta's original settlers are buried here. Check out the Montevista Biblical Gardens. On the west side of the cemetery, along the James Jackson Parkway, is a particularly poignant pet cemetery that is well worth a visit. **Pet Heaven**, established in 1942, is located on the left (if you are heading north), with the driveway just before you cross Proctor Creek. Buried here among the dogs are two squirrels, one duck, two monkeys, and a parrot. Sad (and bad) poetry to departed pets overwhelms the shady area. It is not hard to imagine ghost dogs playing catch and gnawing on bones here amongst the tiny markers. Indeed, there are balls around . . . eternally hopeful dog eyes follow you everywhere waiting for you to finally pick one up and toss it high, beginning the game all over again.

Head for the highest elevations in **Crest Lawn Cemetery**, where the graves are fast being swallowed up by the ubiquitous kudzu vine. Dark and mysterious, Crest Lawn epitomizes the image of the decaying old South. Evangelist George V. Madrigal is buried here. Better known as the Birdman, Madrigal is remembered for his talent for "whistling in tongues." The Birdman took his message and his tunes all over the country before his death in 1994. David Gordon, Jr., who in 1931 became the first (and only) Atlantan to jump off the Empire State Building (and die), is buried at Crest Lawn. More recently, Lester Maddox's mother was buried here. She died in 1995 at the age of 100.

Many, many other cemeteries dot the city of Atlanta.

Some of the smaller ones have been displaced over the years, the bodies being moved to larger graveyards. Others stay where they are while progress rushes around them. Look for a small cluster of headstones in the grassy area of the Cleveland Avenue exit ramp along Interstate 75 South. This is the **Gilbert Memorial Cemetery**, originally a one-acre plot founded in 1861 by Jeremiah F. Gilbert. It was used until the early 20th century, and was destroyed in the 50s by vandals. The cemetery served the surrounding black community. Cross the Interstate carefully to see a monument with names of the buried listed on it; there are also many unmarked graves. Most of this graveyard is underneath the highway. Many churches have their own cemeteries, such as the one at Nancy Creek Church where early pioneer Solomon Goodwin is buried. Another settler, Captain Hezekiah Cheshire (married to one of Solomon Goodwin's daughters), rests in the Benjamin Plaster family cemetery south of the Lindbergh MARTA Station. Cheshire Bridge Road was named after Captain Cheshire.

The **Decatur Cemetery** should be included in any jaunt to that city. Situated north of Ponce de Leon Avenue off Commerce Drive (downtown Decatur), this cemetery has several interesting inhabitants. One is Dr. Thomas Chivers, a poet and friend of Edgar Allen Poe. Each claimed the other plagiarized his work. Martha Mitchell's source of inspiration for *Gone With the Wind* was an earlier book, *Life in Dixie During the War*, written by Decatur Cemetery resident Mary Gay. The Richardson Family, murdered by their wife and mother, rest here all together in the new section. Under a huge shady tree rests Bukumbo, a 15-year-old African, brought back here by Missionaries, whose stone reads "our little black pal of the white soul." A mystery surrounds a large marker labelled the "Marble Hill Sunday School," with over 25 graves of young children. It is not known who they were, how they died, or when it all happened.

Nearby at the Avondale Mall is a large granite monolithic structure, built by developers to surround and protect the Crowley family cemetery. The cemetery is in the parking lot. The Crowleys settled that area in 1802. Between the Decatur Cemetery and the Avondale Mall are many good thrift stores.

(above) Receiving Vault, Westview; (below) Book Crematorium, Greenwood

Westview, Greenwood, Crest Lawn, Hollywood, and the Pet Cemetery are all located near one another and could be visited in a single afternoon. The Montgomery Family Cemetery might be added to a trip to Standing Peachtree, Southview to the Civil Rights Tour, and Oakland as a tour all to itself.

75

# Chapter 14
# Close Encounters

**A**tlanta is largely a practical, no nonsense, slap your hands together and get the job done kind of town. When the unexplainable erupts through the surface of reality, doubters are as quick to deny as believers are to affirm.

Did six-toed giants once walk the Peachtree Trail? Evidence in Union County says yes. Was Panola Mountain a center of occult activity in DeKalb County? Was Christ's face seen swimming in tomato sauce on a Pizza Hut billboard? Or does the Blessed Virgin Mary appear monthly to a rural housewife in Conyers? *Sideways Atlanta* invites you to explore these and many other incidences of the unexplained.

Pilgrims arrive by the tens of thousands on the thirteenth day of every month at a farm in **Conyers**, a small town east of Atlanta on I-20. On May 13, 1993, 35,000 people disembarked from countless tour busses from as far away as Miami. Despite heavy thunderstorm activity over the area, these thousands of believers stayed to hear the words of the Blessed Virgin Mary spoken through the mouth of ordinary housewife Nancy Fowler. At exactly noon, the crowd, which surrounds the Fowler farmhouse, quiets. A priest begins the mass recitation of the rosary, stopping when the Virgin begins speaking to Nancy, who is inside with a core group of supporters. Only Nancy can hear what the Virgin has to say. While she is speaking to Nancy, pilgrims outside are pointing their cameras to the clouds; sometimes the blessed mother's image is recorded on film. After the Virgin leaves, Nancy's voice over the crackling loudspeakers relays the message: Pray. Everyone must pray. There is danger everywhere but prayer will heal the world.

A nearby pole barn has been converted to a bookstore, selling the story of the apparitions. Choose your door carefully . . . each entryway sells books in a different language. Pilgrims may camp in the 180-acre area which includes various shrines, a well of holy water, and a trek through field and woods to "Holy Hill." The Virgin's monthly visits began in October of 1990 and continue to this day.

To visit the site, drive east on I-20 to Conyers. Turn north on route 138. On your left, you will pass a religious supply store, worth a visit to stock up on information and souvenirs. This is also an excellent bookstore selling books on the many other apparitions and miracles worldwide. The store is located directly across the street from a pair of large, guitar wielding statues guarding the gates to an auto center. These statues were originally Reebok promo pieces. Continue north on route 138 to White Road and turn left. For more information, call Our Loving Mother's Children at 922-8885.

Head back into Atlanta and scan billboards for religious images. Many people saw Christ swimming in tomato sauce on a **Pizza Hut billboard** along Memorial Drive at Village Square Street (DeKalb County). Take a side trip to **Panola Mountain**, rumored to be a hotbed of occult activity in the area (18 miles southeast of Atlanta on route 155).

Back in Atlanta, a visit to the **Hare Krishna temple** on Ponce de Leon might be in order to help stretch your mind to encompass yet another reality. Situated just east of Moreland at 1287 Ponce, the temple hosts a variety of activities including festivals, street parades, and dancing. Call 373-4819 for information.

The Hare Krishnas are interested in UFO activities, and in the connections they find in ancient Vedic texts. A UFO enthusiast would likely find lectures and information at one of the temple's festivals, or s/he could contact ETIP (Extraterrestrial Telepathic Intelligence Phenomenon) at 986-0802 to learn more about UFO abductees and abductee research.

In 1953 a space alien was collected on Highway 78 near Austell (west of Atlanta). Three Atlantans claimed to have seen a flying saucer, chased it down, and killed one of the aliens as it tried to get away. Examination of the corpse revealed the alien to look disturbingly like a shaved **rhesus monkey**, which is just what it turned out to be!

In 1960, a **silver box** came screaming out of the sky to bury itself twelve feet deep in a bean patch inside the Atlanta Penitentiary Farm. Traveling from the east at a twelve-degree angle, the object hissed and exploded, sending up a fifty-foot column of sulfur smelling smoke. The military later claimed the object was a fake bomb used to train pilots to drop real ones.

A **mysterious creature** appeared, attacked, and clawed 16-year-old Larry Peters along Fellwood Road (South Fulton County) in 1966. Neither a dog nor a cat, the creature promptly disappeared.

Could this be one of the creatures responsible for the **mysterious cow killings** that began one year later, occuring all over the U.S.? Nearby Fyffe, Alabama, in the northeast corner of the state, has become a very dangerous place for cows to live. One rumor speculated a swamp ape was responsible for the dozens of mutilated bovines turning up. That does not adequately explain the fact that body parts had been removed, bloodlessly, from the cattle in a surgical fashion, with udders, eyes, tongues, and hearts among the parts missing. Fyffe was declared the "UFO Capital of Alabama" in 1989 after several sitings there; however, residents are divided between being convinced the mutilators are alien, or suspecting the abundance of helicopters and furtive men in suits to be evidence of the work of our own U.S. government.

Feeling a bit nervous? It's time for a trip to **Rondos!** Established in 1944 at 171 Mitchell Street, near the State Capitol in downtown Atlanta, Rondo's is your headquarters for voodoo, occult, and religious supplies, from "confuse your enemy" sprays to mental cleansing soaps and love oils, to statues of patron saints of money, power, or luck. Most products claim, in very small type, not to have supernatural powers, but who could not believe, just a little, in the face of the collective strength of the volume of possibilities this unimposing little shop offers?

It's the real thing. We know it.

Conyers, Georgia
May 13, 1993

# Chili Evans

Exotic dancer Chili Evans committed suicide on August 20, 1960, by driving her car at 100 mph. into the underpass at Pryor Street on the Interstate 75/85.  Also known as Marguerette Suzanne Galento, Chili was the mother of four and wife of professional wrestler Spider Galento.

Chili Evans performed at many of Atlanta's top night clubs, including the **Harem Club** at 26 Pine Street.  Originally opening in 1946 as the elegant Club 26, it has  also been known as the Gypsy Room, the House of Dolls, and Club Ebony.  It was torn down in preparation for the 1996 Olympics.  She had performed at the Harem Club the night she died, crying between sets.  Her co-workers tried desperately to cheer her up to no avail.  The dancer stated, "I know of a beautiful brick wall that I am going to drive my car into at 120 miles per hour."

*Sideways Atlanta*, in an unprecedented gesture of homage to our favorite stripper, bought a brick for the walk in Atlanta's Olympic Park.  Inscribed with Chili's name and date of her death, we feel it is a poetic remembrance of her fascination with those "beautiful brick walls."

Chili Evans is buried in an unmarked grave in **College Park Cemetery** on Virginia Avenue near the airport.  Visit **Barbecue Kitchen** (1437 Virginia) for hot barbecue and lots of vegetables or **Spondivets** (1219 Virginia) for good burgers in a thatched roof, open air, Hawaiian motif.  Across from Barbeque Kitchen is a **Holiday Inn**.  The west side rooms provide a good view of the cemetery and of planes taking off.

The Whaling Wall

The World of Coca-Cola

# Chapter 15
# **Downtown**

**W**e might just as well start at Five Points and spiral outward through this densely packed area of interest, not to mention population and traffic congestion. Downtown Atlanta is roughly bounded by Interstates 75/85 on the east, I-20 to the south, Northside Drive (west), and Ponce de Leon Avenue (north).

Parking and driving is always difficult here, if only for the large number of one-way streets. We recommend you take MARTA to Five Points and walk. Our favorite parking garage is on Carnegie Way, behind Macy's (Peachtree & Ellis). Watch out, Ellis is a one-way street, going away from the parking garage! Park and cross Peachtree to the MARTA station, and take the train one stop to Five Points. You could walk it by going straight down Peachtree, but save your feet. If you insist on driving this tour, a Sunday morning might be the only practical time to attempt it.

**Underground Atlanta**

When you exit from the Five Points MARTA station, you will be just west of the actual Five Points. Go east on Alabama to Underground Atlanta, which should technically be called Understreet Atlanta, where the city got its start. Underground Atlanta is a huge commercial sprawl of shops and restaurants, not tasteless but somewhat distracting. It is the site of the original **Zero Mile Post** set by the railroad in 1850. At that time, all railroad lines merged at two terminal buildings, later at Union Station. Field Hospitals were set up here during the Battle of Atlanta; here is where Scarlett came to look for help in birthin' a baby.

After the War Between the States, bridges and viaducts were built over the railroad tracks to prevent people and mules from being hit by trains. So many were built that eventually the shops were forced to begin doing business from their second floors. New buildings and roads eventually sealed off the original streets and old Atlanta went truly underground, or understreet, as it were. In 1968, part of the lower level became an entertainment center. Criticized as being too dark and dank, it was at least felt to be somewhat authentic, but it closed in 1981. In 1989, Underground Atlanta was restored as an upscale shopping mall, with development both in underground and aboveground Underground Atlanta.

Work your way around (from Alabama turn left on Peachtree) to the front entrance of the complex. Broad stairs lead past fountains, waterfalls, and interesting sculptural figures down into a dark, cavelike area lined with pushcarts and vendors. At the bottom of the stairs look for a **lampost**, standing by itself. In 1863, during the shelling of Atlanta, a shell ricocheted off this post, hitting the leg of Negro barber Solomon Luckie, who later died of his wound. The lampost was kept in City Hall until it was returned to its original site in 1880. The United Daughters of the Confederacy dedicated it to a Confederate general in 1919. In 1939, to help celebrate the premier of *Gone With the Wind*, the lamp was given the gift of eternal life by the Atlanta Gas Light Company. It stands now as a monument to the "Eternal Flame of the Confederacy."

The Underground Atlanta area extends from Peachtree to Pryor to Central, bisected by Alabama both above and below ground. Inside Underground, you can still see original brick, stone walls, and cast iron columns. Most of this area has been restored, so little of the original remains. It is worth walking through to see the photographs of old Atlanta displayed; a guide sheet is available at one of the information centers. The Atlanta History Center has moved its branch office to **Heritage Row**, on upper Alabama Street.

From Peachtree (on your right as you look down into the entrance) to Pryor, the stretch along underground Alabama Street is the area once known as **Humbug Square**, meeting place of medicine men, con artists, magicians, and evangelists. Cynics claim this area is still known as Humbug Square. Nightclub **Dante's Down the Hatch** sits at the underground corner of Alabama and Pryor.

This was the corner where an old jail stood. It was so rickety, friends of the jailed could simply lift up the corner of the building to let their cronies out. This is also where the **field hospital** was set up during the Battle of Atlanta.

**President Woodrow Wilson's law firm** (Renick & Wilson) was located in Underground in 1883. **Kenney's Alley** is named for P.J. Kenny, a saloon owner who died at the first Georgia State Fair in a mock jousting tournament. Kenny's establishment was located on Alabama near the corner of Whitehall (now Peachtree).

The freight depot is located at the eastern end at Central. The oldest building in Underground Atlanta, it was partly destroyed by fire in 1935. At this end of the complex is also the site of the Zero Mile Post. The exact spot is covered over now by the Central Avenue viaduct, but a plaque commemorates the general area.

As you step out of the dimly lit world of old Atlanta and your eyes slowly clear, you might need to slap the side of your head (and those of your companions, just for fun) to be assured you are not having a vision, seeing a mirage, experiencing a flashback . . . the giant whales you see here are not an illusion! The 27,000 square foot mural was painted by artist Robert Thomas Wyland in 1993. It is a very surrealistic moment to take in the **Whaling Wall**, then look beyond it to see the whales must be guarding the entrance to **The World of Coca-Cola**.

Coca-Cola was invented in Atlanta by Dr. John Pemberton as a headache remedy. Pemberton was also creator of the Globe of Flower Cough Syrup, Indian Queen Hair Dye, and the French Wine of Coca--Ideal Tonic. Coca-Cola did not take hold until a cranky customer with a headache asked for the syrup to be mixed with soda water. The rest is history, and all the Coca-Cola history you want AND more is waiting for you at this museum singlemindedly dedicated to one commercial product. Samples of Coca-Cola flavors from around the world are available at the end of the tour; be sure to try as many as you can. Some are exceptionally foul and nasty! The World of Coca-Cola is thoroughly, joyfully, quintessentially bustin' out all over American, and not to be missed.

The World of Coca-Cola is open every day except major holidays. Call 676-5151 for hours and reservations.

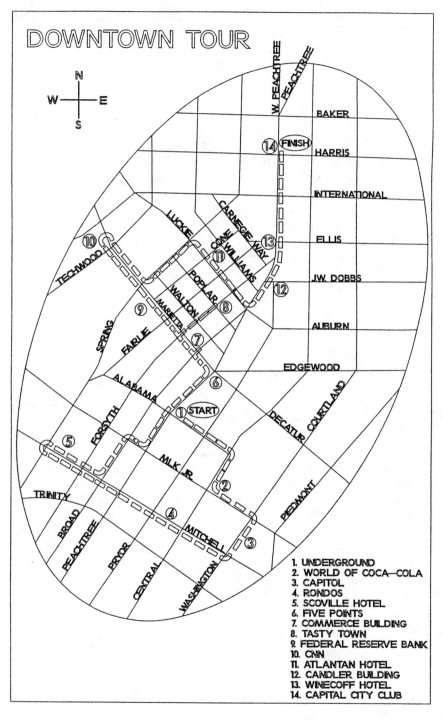

# DOWNTOWN TOUR

N
W · E
S

W. PEACHTREE
PEACHTREE
BAKER
14 FINISH HARRIS
INTERNATIONAL
LUCKIE
CARNEGIE WAY
PINE
WILLIAMS
ELLIS
13
10
TECHWOOD
11
J.W. DOBBS
POPLAR
12
WALTON
9
MARIETTA
8
SPRING
FAIRLIE
7
AUBURN
ALABAMA
EDGEWOOD
6
1 START
DECATUR
COURTLAND
FORSYTH
5
MLK JR.
TRINITY
2
PIEDMONT
BROAD
4
PEACHTREE
MITCHELL
3
PRYOR
CENTRAL
WASHINGTON

1. UNDERGROUND
2. WORLD OF COCA—COLA
3. CAPITOL
4. RONDOS
5. SCOVILLE HOTEL
6. FIVE POINTS
7. COMMERCE BUILDING
8. TASTY TOWN
9. FEDERAL RESERVE BANK
10. CNN
11. ATLANTAN HOTEL
12. CANDLER BUILDING
13. WINECOFF HOTEL
14. CAPITAL CITY CLUB

"Sideways Special" Map of Downtown Atlanta

85

## The Capitol Area

From the World of Coca-Cola at Martin Luther King, Jr. Drive, begin your walk to the State Capitol. You will be just south of the corner of Decatur and Courtland, site of Atlanta's red-light district of the 1880s. Do you think Coca-Cola's big red sign of lights commemorates this? At the time of the 1896 accidental burning of the **Markham House Hotel** (one block to your left on Decatur), more than 10,000 people thronged the street, competing with horses from the burning horse stables, Chinese immigrants from the burning laundry, Jewish storekeepers from their burning businesses, and of course, the prostitutes from their burning houses of ill repute. Burning, sparking telegraph wires and trolley lines added to the drama of the evening.

On the other side of Martin Luther King, Jr. Drive (MLK) is the **Shrine of the Immaculate Conception**, the oldest Catholic church in Atlanta. The original church was built on the site in 1848 and escaped Sherman and the burning of Atlanta. It was rebuilt in 1872, and again in 1984. The crypt of Father Thomas O'Reilly, the priest who saved the church from burning by the Yankees, is in the basement and may be visited by making an advance appointment. The rest of the Shrine is open for public perusal except during Masses. Call 521-1866 for information or appointments.

At Washington (this street is also Courtland), turn right. On your left is the **Georgia State Capitol**, its dome covered with gold from the North Georgia gold mines near Dahlonega. The State Capitol houses the **Georgia State Museum of Science and Industry** on the fourth floor. It boasts a two-headed snake and a two-headed calf. Paintings portraying Georgia Governors are also located here. Be sure to check out the one of former governor Lester Maddox. Pictured at his desk, he is standing next to a photograph of his wife, two peaches, and a dead fish wrapped in the *Atlanta Constitution.*

Nearby at 300 Capitol Avenue (turn left on Mitchell, right on Capitol) are the **Georgia State Archives**, a repository of history for researchers and the curious. The monolithic building looks inaccessible; in reality you only need a picture ID. A rumor has this whole building dropping neatly into an already prepared hole in case of a nuclear explosion. The Archives overlook the intersection of I-75/85 and I-20. This snarl of superhighway was built right over the house of **Julia Force**, curry-deranged killer of her two sisters. South of the Archives is the **Fulton County Stadium**, where Hank Aaron hit baseballs and the Beatles played music. In the early 1900s this was a thriving red-light district. It was also the home to Atlanta's Sephardic Jewish community.

If you turn right on Mitchell (from Washington), you will see the Atlanta City Hall on your left. It has a great ornate lobby and an information center.

After your close brush with governmental bureaucracies, and with a politician or two if you are *very* unlucky, a visit to **Rondo's** might be just the ticket to cleanse your aura. Go up Mitchell toward Peachtree (if driving, this is one-way and you'll have to go around). Cross Central and look for Rondo's on the right at 171 Mitchell. Established in 1944, Rondo's is the best place in town we know of to buy "Confuse Your Enemies" spray, a must for everyone's office desk. Dream books, attractant and repellant oils, curse and anti-curse powders . . . all your aspirations good & bad can find a solution at Rondo's.

Continue on Mitchell to Spring Street. You are in the **Hotel Row** area, which once housed four hotels and various commercial buildings. On your right, at Mitchell and Forsyth is **Concordia Hall**, built in 1892. Look up to its second and third stories to see interesting architectural details of the oldest building in this block. The hall was originally a Jewish community center. The block between Forsyth and Spring Streets features the Gordon Hotel, the Scoville Hotel, and the Sylvan Hotel. The **Terminal Hotel**, which burned in 1938, killing 34 persons, was located at the northeast corner of Spring and Mitchell Streets. These hotels were built near the Atlanta Terminal (train) Station, and declined in the 50s and 60s, especially after the Terminal Station was torn down. The most interesting of the hotels is the **Scoville Hotel** (formerly the Marion Hotel). Entering the lobby is like stepping into a 1920s time warp. Most of the other hotels have been altered to create offices and apartments. Go back down Mitchell to Broad Street (go left), take Broad to MLK (go right), and MLK back to Peachtree. This route will take you through the original downtown shopping area. There is still some interesting architecture here, with storefronts and good old signs from the 1940s and 50s.

Rondo's

Site of the Zero Mile Marker outside of
Underground Atlanta

## Five Points and Peachtree Street

Once you pass Underground Atlanta, look to your left for 10 Peachtree Street (now a fashion and gift mart). This is where Robert A. Crawford brokered slaves, buying and selling his merchandise for distribution all over the south.

One block more and you are at Five Points, junction of two ancient trails; now it is the intersection of Marietta, Peachtree, Edgewood, and Decatur Streets. This is where **Scarlett's lumberyard** was, where the **1906 race riots** took place (also Decatur & Pryor, Marietta & Forsyth), and where the **first Coca-Colas were sold** at Jacob's drugstore. Look for the plaque commemorating the notorious **Murrel's Row** on the side of the Olympia Building facing Five Points. The **Kimball House Hotel**, pet project of Reconstructionist entrepreneur H.I. Kimball, was located here, one block east on Decatur at Pryor and Kimball Way.

Negro barber **Alonzo Herndon** had his first job here at a barbershop at 11 Marietta in 1882. Walk up Marietta to Broad Street. The **Commerce Building**, at 34 Broad, was originally built as a parking deck for the **C&S Building** (now Nations Bank at 35 Broad). The Commerce Building ended up with stores on the bottom floor, the parking deck in the middle, and the members-only Commerce Club on the top floors. The side of the building displays a metal rendering of the State of Georgia by artist Julian Harris, done in 1959, the same year the building was constructed. Check the Nations Bank's grand lobby which features Georgia marbles. Back on Marietta, continue towards the **Henry Grady statue** sitting in the middle of the street. Grady was part owner and editor of the *Atlanta Constitution*, civic leader, and great orator. **Woodrow Wilson's law firm** was located at the intersection of Forsyth and Marietta, and one of the first stores in Atlanta, Johnson & Thrasher, was located here in 1839. Turn right on Forsyth Street to see the **Healy Building** on your right. Built in 1913, this building has a wonderful atrium. Be sure to check out the barbershop. If you are very lucky, you might see Bill in there getting his hair cut! The Healy Building is at 57 Forsyth. Across the street, at 56 Forsyth, is the **U.S. 11th District Court of Appeals**, an interesting looking building that was originally a post office. **Tasty Town**, at 67 Forsyth, an old restaurant/diner, might be a good place to stop for a snack. Try their apple pie ala mode or "our reputation" (chopped steak). Tell them, "I want a reputation, please!"

Return to Marietta and walk two more blocks to where

Cone deadends into Marietta. This is where the **Monetary Museum** is, located in the Federal Reserve Bank. There is a sculpture of a big eagle out front. **The Federal Reserve Bank**, one of twelve in the country, requires you to sign in, present a picture I.D., and wear a clip tag for your visit to the museum. The museum is VERY dry. On display is Confederate money and a gold bar weighing 395.45 troy ounces. The bar is 99.8% pure gold and is worth somewhere in the neighborhood of $150,000; the Confederate money is worthless. Be sure and take home an envelope of shredded money as a souvenir!

**John Pemberton**, inventor of the Coca-Cola syrup, lived at Marietta and Spring Street. The whole area is parking lots now, but you can still get a Coke at **Cesare's Corner Cafe** right at Marietta and Spring.

One block past Spring you will cross Techwood and see on your left the **CNN Center**, home of Ted Turner's CNN 24-hour news station and the Turner Broadcasting empire. A CNN tour is essential to a good, satisfying visit of Atlanta. Tickets must be bought in advance on the day of your tour. Each tour is limited to 20 people; it is best to get there early, especially during the busy tourist seasons. The long escalator you take at the start of the tour used to lead to the World of Sid and Marty Krofft: vaudeville puppeteers whose 5-story amusement park was a unique, highly interactive experience. Some might remember Sid & Marty for such Saturday morning treats as H.R. Puffenstuff.

Ted took over where Sid & Marty left off. The CNN tour will give you the oppportunity to see your favorite newscasters walking around eating apples, slurping milkshakes, and reporting the news live, 24 hours a day. It is an extremely interesting tour. Wear blue for your tour; you'll find out why once you get there!

The **CNN Movie Theatres** are good places to see horror movies (the regular clientele is very verbal!). The **World Congress Center** is situated right in back of CNN on International Boulevard. Our favorite restaurant, **Thelma's**, once stood at 190 Luckie. Edged out by construction for the 1996 Olympic Park, she is now housed near Georgia Tech at 768 Marietta Street. Her Brunswick Stew is perfect.

Back outside CNN, go down Marietta and go left on Spring to Williams to the site of **Walton Spring**, a resort and gathering area similar to the Ponce de Leon Springs Park. This is now the American Hotel. It was at Walton Spring that Antonio Maquino, who ran a concession stand there, invented the world's first Ferris Wheel.

Walk back to Luckie, turn left, and head for Peachtree. When you get to Cone Street, see the **Atlantan Hotel**, where at one time a floor was devoted to a minimum security prison. An Atlanta Cracker, Hugh Casey, committed suicide here in 1951, while talking on the phone with his wife.

At Forsyth and Luckie is the **Old Rialto Theatre**, saved from destruction and restored. It is now the Music Building for Georgia State University. As you walk back toward Peachtree Street, you will see the **1897 Flatiron Building**, one of Atlanta's first commercial buildings, right in front of you. At Peachtree, two blocks to your right, you can see where Alonzo Herndon had his barbershop, at 66 Peachtree Street. The building, which also borders on Broad Street, is slated for removal. Look across Woodruff Park to see the beginning of "Sweet" Auburn Avenue.

Turn left on Peachtree and walk up to 140, the **1911 Hillyer Building**. It is located adjacent to **Margaret Mitchell Square** and a public artwork/fountain, rarely turned on, and repository of much litter. It is Atlanta's thinnest building, only 21 feet wide!

Across the street is the **Asa G. Candler Building**, completed in 1906. Seventeen stories high, the building contains statues of his parents in the lobby. Panels of artwork and busts of classical artists, writers, and musicians grace the outside of the building. Look for the hound dogs decorating the Wesley Dobbs side of the building, and find the profile of Buffalo Bill Cody. The Candler Building was built on the site of the original Wesley Chapel.

The **Downtown Annex of the High Museum of Art** is located at the corner of Houston and Peachtree in the Georgia Pacific Building. This is the site of Loew's Grand Theatre, where *Gone With the Wind* premiered in 1939. The High Museum houses the Folk Art and Photography galleries, and is open 10-5 Monday-Saturday. Phone 577-6940 for information.

Across Margaret Mitchell Square, where Carnegie Way meets Forsyth and Peachtree, is the **Atlanta Public Library**, where Margaret Mitchell did much of her research for *Gone With the Wind* and where Bill researched *Sideways Atlanta*. Continue up Peachtree on the left (west) side of the street. Here is the site of **"The House that Jack Built."** When Jasper N. Smith built this structure in 1889, he had two stone tablets made bearing information on his house and his philosophy of life. When the house was sold, it was stipulated that the tablets would always stay on display. They now decorate one of the entrances to the Peachtree MARTA Station. This station once boasted the longest escalator in the world. It is still pretty long! The **Wynne-Claughton Building and the Winecoff Hotel** are on your left at Ellis. The Winecoff, at the corner of Peachtree and Ellis, was the scene of a spectacular fire in 1946, killing 119 guests, including Margaret "Lucious" Nichols, a former Miss Atlanta, and Mr. W. Frank Winecoff himself. Local real estate mogul Bruce Weinkauf is no relation to W. Frank. Ironically, the hotel was billed as fireproof. In frantic attempts to save themselves, victims threw themselves out their windows, only to die on the street below, right in front of **Charlie's Sandwich Shop** on Ellis Street, our favorite place in Atlanta to get grits. Charlie's is also the home of the 37-cent large cup of coffee. The Wynne-Claughton Building (now the Carnegie Building) is behind the Winecoff Hotel on Carnegie Way. It was once the State Headquarters for the Ku Klux Klan. Their offices were located in rooms 1118-1122.

Continue up Peachtree to Harris. You will pass **Macy's** on the left. Macy's arrived in Atlanta in 1925 and signalled the move of the retail district from the Five Points area to the north. The six-story building is the height of an 11-story building: Macy's Atlanta is the world's tallest 6-story building! Walk through the lobby of the store. Across from Macy's at 191 Peachtree Tower are two huge light fixtures which in the daylight, look like giant jeweled turds! On the left, the **Westin Peachtree Hotel**, designed by John Portman with a revolving restaurant at the top, is a good place to get a nice view of the city without doing much work. The hotel sits on the site of the first governor's mansion built in Atlanta, first occupied by Scallawag governor Rufus B. Bullock.

The corner of International and Peachtree features both the **Hardrock Cafe and Planet Hollywood. The Cornerstone Building** on the southeast corner, has interesting batwing designs along the top. Look down International Boulevard (to the right) two blocks to see the area where original settler Hardy Ivy built his first house. Left, at International (Walton) and Spring is The **American(a) Hotel**, a great example of early 60s (1962) architecture. The **Welcome to the South Center** at International and Spring pipes out southern music to entice visitors to come inside and learn more about the region.

At Harris, two blocks to your right, was the site of the Atlanta City Brewery, which burned in 1880. New Year's Eve

1990, as the Big Peach fell from the tower downtown, revelers at the **Marriott Marquis** went on a rampage, trashing the hotel, and spraying guests with fire extinguishers. Plants and chairs were thrown off the indoor balconies, forcing guests below to hide under tables. This hotel also has a scary fast elevator ride. The elevator shoots you up through what looks like the belly of a whale! Harris and Courtland is also now the site of the **Hilton Hotel**, where **serial killer Henry Hodges** killed his last victim, strangling a visitor from North Carolina with a curtain cord. Hodges was caught when he and his girlfriend Trina Brown used the victim's car and credit cards to travel back to North Carolina where the police were waiting. The Hilton is also where **Rob Lowe**, during the 1988 Democratic Convention, was inspired to create his very own sex video. The **Hyatt Regency Hotel**, at the corner of Harris and Peachtree, was where British journalist Sandy Fawkes spent a few days in 1974 dallying with **serial killer John Paul Knowles**, who did not end up killing anyone in Atlanta. The bar they hung out at, the **Polaris Lounge**, is a revolving restaurant with a blue top that was once the most prominent feature in the Atlanta skyline. Now it is dwarfed by recently constructed skyscrapers. Across from the Hyatt Regency is the **Capital City Club**, founded in 1883, a hub of social activity in Atlanta. The Club was founded by a group of bored young men who met for entertainment and activity in the Kimball house. The Club rapidly grew, moving into its present quarters in 1911, where, among other things, members kept liquor in lockers during prohibition and slot machines were provided for entertainment. A plaque inside commemorates Jacques Futrelle, the only Atlantan who died on the Titanic. Entertaining presidents, confederates, and visitors from all over the world, the Capital City Club hosts dinners, balls, summer tea dances, and debutante activities. Arthur Murray taught dancing on the Roof Garden in 1919, from where you could see Stone Mountain, 16 miles in the distance.

Our tour ends here. You are only a block from the Peachtree Center MARTA station (it will be on your left as you walk down Peachtree towards Five Points). Another MARTA station is located across the street from the Winecoff Hotel, and the parking garage is behind Macy's.

# Chapter 16
# Midtown

**M**idtown Atlanta encompasses the areas between Northside Drive (on the west), Monroe (east), I-85 (north), and I-75/85 (south). If you are approaching this tour from downtown, simply take Peachtree north into Midtown. Peachtree will split and turn into Peachtree and West Peachtree at West Peachtree. Get it? Nobody does. There are **27 Peachtrees** (roads, circles, avenues, etc.) not including plazas, parks, and points. That there is but one venerable, original Peachtree Street is of small comfort to the confused visitor, especially as the one venerable, original Peachtree Street eventually turns into Peachtree Road, and later, Peachtree Industrial Boulevard. And remember, it was once all the Peachtree Trail! So! As you are driving north on Peachtree Street, look for the fork in the road and bear right to remain on Peachtree Street. In 1898 **gold was discovered** at the southeast corner of Peachtree and Baker Streets (just before the fork). In 1931, when the home of Dr. J.R. Hopkins was torn down, it was again checked for gold, but only a bit was found. There are a few other interesting buildings right here where the Peachtrees split. **One Peachtree Center** features two giant statues of naked women dancing. There was a great deal of controversy over the women when the sculpture first was installed, but the dancers remain. The **Sacred Heart Church** was built in 1897. The **Imperial Hotel** is abandoned, but still standing, at 355 Peachtree. Built in 1910, it has steel studs for fireproofing. Inside was the **Domino Lounge**, a premier strip club of the 50s and 60s.

When the Peachtrees cross I-75/85 for the first time, you are entering Midtown. West Peachtree meets Peachtree again a few miles north at Pershing Point. Right after that, Peachtree Street crosses the Interstate again and you have left Midtown.

Meanwhile, back where the Peachtrees originally split,

head north. You will turn left on Alexander Street (Ralph McGill Boulevard is on the right). The **First United Methodist Church of Atlanta** (1903) is at this corner. Go to West Peachtree and turn right. You will pass between the two sides of the MARTA Civic Center Station as you cross the Interstate. On the right will be Pine Street, home of the former **Harem Club** (which had many other names). This is where our favorite stripper Chili Evans was working the night she drove her car into a brick wall. The infamous Blaze Starr also put in appearances at the Harem Club.

On your left, you will get a good view of the **Baltimore Block**, Atlanta's first apartment complex. Built in 1885, the block originally consisted of fourteen identical row houses, 18 feet wide and 70 feet deep. Three stories tall, the structures were separate buildings joined at the top by a long white cornice. The units also boasted the first central heating in Atlanta through a vent system radiatiing from a first floor fireplace. At first, the houses on Baltimore Block attracted fashionable society, but gradually went out of style, experiencing serious deterioration until the 30s, when artists moved in to use the buildings as studios, antique shops, and a community tearoom. In addition to the artists, photographers, landscape architects, and interior designers worked to improve the row of houses, which had shrunk to ten after an oil company built at the corner of Spring Street.

Turn right on Prescott from West Peachtree to return to (the original) Peachtree Street. The **Crawford Long Hospital** is on the left, named after the discoverer of anesthesia. Look for the **Atlanta Museum** on the right (east) side of the street at 537. The building is the Rufus M. Rose House, one of the few remaining grand homes along Peachtree. It was built in 1900. Rumored to be the repository of such memorabilia as a Japanese Bomber, a lock of Napolean's hair, and a collection of Hitleriana, this museum keeps such irregular hours we have been unable to visit and see for ourselves (yet!). Try calling 872-8233. **Mick's Restaurant**, at 577 Peachtree, is a fine and rowdy place to eat.

At Ponce, you can go left to have a bite to eat at the **Varsity** (two blocks). You will pass the **Southern Bell Building**, whose structure creates a wind tunnel known as "the" place to go in Atlanta during an approaching thunderstorm. The corner of Ponce and Peachtree boasts the **Fox Theatre** and the **Georgian Terrace** (including the Road to Tara Museum). Tours of the Fox are scheduled through the Atlanta History Center; allow an hour for a good look at the

Road to Tara Museum.

Continue north. Eight hundred Peachtree is where **Oliver Hardy** (Laurel and Hardy) spent some of his boyhood. The Villager Lodge, a Vegas-style hotel, is on your left at 870. Formerly the **Cabana**, this hotel has a magnificent curved stairway where we are sure you will want to be photographed (after donning lovely evening clothes, of course). Doris Day owned the hotel in the 60s. It was used for scenes during the filming of *Cannonball Run*. Indoor gardens surround a curved mural painting in three parts: "The Transcendence of Venus." The Scarlett Ballroom hosts floor to ceiling paintings from *Gone With the Wind*. Outside, fountains and classical statues rise from behind formal box hedges. You can still see the putting green right on Peachtree. Walk to the back of the hotel and stand at the rail in the rear of the elevated parking lot. From this vantage point, look south to see **the William Greene Raoul residence**, built in 1892. One of the area's last giant mansions, the front is now stores. The back area is partly burned, but you can still see the servant's quarters and the stables. Look back onto the street below. This is **Cypress Street**, where in the evenings, you can see a parade of hustlers. The **Metro Bar**, at Sixth and Cypress, is right in the thick of it all. They feature cookouts on Fridays and Saturdays. From this vantage point you can also see the **Academy of Medicine** (875 West Peachtree), which is on the National Register. Built in 1940, it is a beautiful example of elegant period architecture, and hosts, in the formal entrance, a chandelier used in *Gone With the Wind*. The **Biltmore Hotel**, dating from 1924, is also visible (can't miss it!), as is the **Atlanta Fencing Club** at Seventh and Cypress. Occasionally, fencers must fend off hustlers in dramatic displays of skill. Look carefully to see if anyone is wearing the black mask of Zorro!

Next door to the Cabana is where Jayne Mansfield had her hair done by **Mr. Donald of Atlanta** in 1962. Directly across the street from the Cabana, the **Backstreet Bar** (formerly Funancho's) is where Lynyrd Skynyrd was discovered. The southern redneck anthem "Freebird" was recorded live at the Fox Theatre.

At Peachtree and 10th, you will find a Metro Police Station and the charred remnants of the house in which Margaret Mitchell wrote her classic novel. The house is located right at the corner of 10th and Crescent. Formerly known as **"The Dump"** the Windsor House Apartments are being restored to create a welcome center for the 1996 Olympics. Near the

13th Street intersection is **where Mitchell was struck and killed** by taxi driver Hugh Gravitt.

Tenth Street marks the center of the notorious **"Tight Squeeze"** of 19th century Atlanta. The area between 7th and 14th Streets, known as **"The Strip"** during the 1960s, boasted a Hippie population of up to 35,000. By 1973, all the Hippies were gone.

Turn left and take a quick detour down 14th Street. On the left is a **Gorin's Diner**, 50s style, good for ice cream.

**The Center for Puppetry Arts** is located at 1404 Spring Street. You can't turn right from 14th as Spring is one-way in the wrong direction, but you can go around the block. The Museum features changing exhibits; guided tours are offered with opportunities for hands-on experience. Some remnants of the World of Sid & Marty Krofft are housed here. Call 874-0398 for information on hours and current events.

A really big **sinkhole** appeared near the corner of 14th and Techwood Drive on June 14, 1993. Two people were killed, three cars were destroyed, and one person was swept a mile away when the earth unexpectedly collapsed around a 1915 underground water culvert. To see the actual site check the lower parking lot at the Courtyard by Marriott. Stop in at the **Silver Skillet** on 14th for good food in an authentic 50s atmosphere. Turn right on Francis Street. At the end of the street in this blue collar neighborhood is the **Atlantic Steel Company**, which opened in 1901, and will soon move to Cartersville. **"Big Tom,"** the plant's steam whistle, keeps time for everyone for miles around, ringing at 7, 12, and 6. Turn left on 16th Street and left again on State to return to 14th. At the corner of State and 14th is **Kool Korners**, with excellent Cuban sandwiches.

Cross 14th and enter **Home Park**. This was the neighborhood of Lester P. Maddox: segregationist, restauranteur, philosopher, and Georgia governor. Maddox grew up here. Hunnerkoff Street (German, meaning Chicken Head) is on the left. At 11th is the elementary school Maddox attended. It is now the State Street Academy Apartments. His restaurant, the Pickrick Cafe, was located at 866 Hemphill (State to 10th, go right to Hemphill, go left). The cafe is now a Georgia Tech building. The Pickrick is where Maddox made his stand against segregation in the 1960s, when he stood in the doorway with an ax to prevent blacks from entering. Later, he sold ax handles as souvenirs.

**Georgia Tech** (motto: "I'm a ramblin' wreck from Georgia Tech and a hell of an engineer") created a can of worms-like

roadway system to confuse, we are sure, any visitor, especial-
ly ones from arch-rival UGA (University of Georgia, Athens).
Tech is the resting place of **our mascot, the little dog
Sideways**. Her grave is located just northwest of the
Administration Building.  When State Street deadends at
Ferst, go right.  The road will horseshoe, and you can't miss
the new Olympic natatorium on the right.  When Ferst dead-
ends, turn left on Cherry, and look for the Administration
Building on the right.  Retrace your path back: Ferst, State,
10th.

   **Techwood**, one of Atlanta's and America's original public
housing developments, borders Tech.  Originally called
Tanyard Bottom, Techwood is located between North, Mills,
Williams, and Lovejoy streets.  Archaeologists are digging in
the area, looking for Civil War artifacts.  The Atlanta Rolling
Mill was located there, as were Confederate trenches from the
defense of the city.  It has been recently torn up to build
Olympic dormitories.  You should return to Peachtree Street
via 10th, where you will turn left and pass through Tight
Squeeze once more.

   As you drive towards Peachtree on 10th and cross Spring
Street, notice the **Spring Hill Mortuary** on the left.  Built in
1928, it has "hosted" many notable Atlanta bodies.  Get in the
left lane and go left on West Peachtree.  The brick building on
your left is where James Brown's 70s dance show "Future
Shock" was broadcast.  This is also where Ted Turner's early
studios were located.  Turn right on 11th.  **The Vortex**, on
the corner, has the best burgers in town.  On 11th and
Crescent, behind a record store on the left was the apartment
building where James Earl Ray stayed after shooting the
Reverend Martin Luther King, Jr.  It was then a sort of
halfway house and is now a parking lot.  One block north on
Crescent is the **Scrap Bar**, on the left, decorated with big
welded things.  It is a good place to go for bands.

   Back on Peachtree, just before 14th, you will see the
**Wimbish House** on your left.  This 1898 building, reminis-
cent of a chateau, has been home to the Atlanta Women's
Club since 1919.

   After 14th, the **Woodruff Arts Center** will be on the left.
Housing the Atlanta College of Art, a Performing Arts Center,
and the **High Museum of Art**, this block is a center of high
culture.  In back of the High Museum is **The Castle**, an
example of unusual architecture engulfed by more modern
buildings. Built in 1910 by Ferdinand McMillan, the architectural assemblage with its Corinthian columns, Chinese tur-

rets, and paintings of fairy-tale characters is a great example of postmodern thought well ahead of its time. A parking garage in back of the complex can be found on Lombardy Way. The High Museum was used as an insane asylum in the film, *Manhunter*, prequel to *Silence of the Lambs*. Step inside the building and you'll understand why! **The Reid House**, on the right at 16th, is also known as the Garrison Apartments. Built in 1924, the building has gone condo. Notice the bull skull motifs along the pediment.

Peachtree and West Peachtree come back together at Pershing Point, site of **Al Kooper's Sound of the South** recording studio where Mountain, among others, worked their magic. **Rhodes Hall** (1516 Peachtree on the left), originally was a home designed after a German castle incorporating many other styles, elements, and features to create another example of early inadvertent Postmodern Architecture (see also the Fox Theatre). Rhodes Hall, now administered by the Georgia Trust for Historic Preservation, displays nine panels of stained glass windows depicting the "Rise and Fall of the Confederacy." Call 881-9980 for information on hours and tours.

You are now at the north end of Midtown Atlanta. Just as you cross the Interstate, you will see the Amtrak Station **(Brookwood Station)** on your left; this modest 1917 building is the only place in Atlanta where a person can catch a train anymore, and then, only twice a day. Continue up Peachtree and find yourself in Buckhead, land of the city's rich and famous. We'll avoid Buckhead and just turn right on Peachtree (Circle) to meander around **Ansley Park** for awhile. Ansley's homes date from 1903, when the 376-acre neighborhood was created by Edwin P. Ansley. These fine old homes are now, as then, in one of Atlanta's most fashionable and desirable city neighborhoods and the whole of Ansley Park is on the National Register of Historic Places. W. Frank Winecoff, owner of the ill-fated Winecoff Hotel, had a house on Peachtree Circle till it burned in 1913. Margaret Mitchell's husband John Marsh lived here at 26 Walker Terrace after her death. The Daughters of the Confederacy still have a house here. Try to make your way through Ansley Park to the corner of South Prado and Piedmont. The apartment building here is another place where Margaret Mitchell lived while writing her epic novel. There is a plaque. Legend has it Mitchell burned her early manuscripts in the basement of this building.

Turn left on Piedmont and right into the **Botanical**

**Gardens**. The gardens are located near the north end of **Piedmont Park**, established as a city park in 1904. Before that, it was site of the **1895 Cotton States and International Exposition**. Many beautiful Victorian buildings were built for this great event; none are still standing. The Exposition featured a Great Midway with a ferris wheel, water chutes, and a "Mystic Maze." They competed for attention with the "Streets of Cairo," a "Mexican Village" including bullfights, an ostrich farm, a gold mine, a moorish palace, and "Monkey Paradise." More than a million people visited the Exposition during its three-month life. Parades and band concerts were interspersed throughout the more serious buildings devoted to Transportation, Machinery, Agriculture, Government, and Fine Arts, to name a very few. In a quiet, out of the way corner stood the "Confederate Relics" building. There was even a Negro building and a Women's building. The latter was designed by Pittsburgh, Pennsylvania architect Elsie Mercer. Buffalo Bill performed with his Wild West Show. Master of Ceremonies for the opening was ex-governor Rufus B. Bullock, and among the notable speakers of that evening was Booker T. Washington. John Phillip Sousa's "King Cotton" was the official march of the exposition, and even the Liberty Bell visited, all the way from Philadelphia!

The Botanical Garden isn't quite the Cotton States Exposition, but its lovely grounds are reminiscent of the extravaganza. With many exhibits including Japanese, Iris, Moon, and Drought-Tolerant Gardens, the Atlanta Botanical Garden covers 60 acres. The Fuqua Conservatory is home to tropical, desert, and endangered plants, and the Storza Woods is a hardwood forest protecting many 100-year-old trees. The gardens are a wonderful way to get away from city life and dream about ways to improve your own gardens. Call 876-5859 for info or 875-GROW for the Plant Hotline.

A walk around Piedmont Park itself gives the visitor a look at Atlanta's runners, walkers, skateboarders, etc., and if you are very lucky, croquet players. Enthusiasts of this sport might want to contact **The Atlanta Mallet Club** at 2513 Kingscliff Drive. It is said that rejects of this club can be seen late at night in Midtown Atlanta playing **street croquet**. In **a 1917 airplane demonstration** to show how easy flying was, pilot Walter Carr managed to crash his biplane in front of 10,000 people gathered in Piedmont Park. Amazingly, he survived. "All in a days work," he said, slapping his hands together. Piedmont Park is now being extended into Monroe and Clear Creek Parks (along Piedmont's east side) to create longer biking and jogging trails, and extensive displays of indigenous plants and trees.

Our tour of Midtown ends here. To get back downtown, go west on 14th and south on Peachtree. If you're now going on the Tour of Ponce, begin at the Fox Theatre, corner of Peachtree and Ponce de Leon Avenue.

The Biltmore, seen from the Villager Lodge (formerly the Cabana)

The Silver Skillet

Lawn Art at the Cabana with
the William Greene Raoul residence ruins in the background

# Jayne Mansfield
# visits Atlanta

Glamorous actress Jayne Mansfield made several visits to Atlanta during the early 60s. In 1961, Jayne and her husband Mickey Hargitay's trip to Miami was delayed at the airport for several hours due to bad weather. A devout fan, who had been waiting all day for her big chance, invited the couple to rest at her nearby home. She was an autograph hound who often spent many hours at the airport, hoping for a signature. JoAnne and Buddy Player, of 877 Virginia Avenue, apartment 15, sat up drinking coffee for three hours while Jayne and her husband slept. JoAnne gave Jayne a painting of an Oscar she had done before taking them back to the airport. It is not known if the Players ever visited Jayne in Hollywood, or met Mansfield on other trips to Atlanta.

In 1962, Mansfield was in Atlanta to open two Thrift City stores, one in Marietta and one at 2176 Bankhead Highway. The Marietta store is closed; the Bankhead Highway store is now a K-Mart. Jayne did a televised one-hour tour of the store, which aired on Wednesday, August 15, 1962 on WLWA (ABC), competing with "Wagon Train," (NBC), and "Alvin and the Chipmunks" (CBS).

After missing her first date to open the glamorous Copa Atlanta (later, Whiskey-A-Go-Go) at 114 Ponce de Leon, the actress performed a week later, "a little off in the timing," perhaps due to lack of rehearsal. She did have time to have Mr. Donald of Atlanta do her hair and to pose for photographers with a little dog named Gallina. Coiffures by Donald was located at 884 Peachtree (now an office building), right next door to the Cabana (now the Villager Lodge).

Jayne's last visit to Atlanta was marred by the tragic loss of a diamond bracelet of great monetary and sentimental value. Happily, it was later found under the back seat of a cab and returned.

# Chapter 17
## Sounds of the South

**A**tlanta is no Memphis. Great traditions and wellsprings of inspiration never took hold in this busy, activity-oriented city. It is a place where performers are appreciated; the Beatles performed here on August 18, 1965, Elvis sent out for food at the Varsity whenever he was in town, and the B52s and the Talking Heads played at the Georgian Terrace's Agora Ballroom.

**Elton John** lives here, part time. **Gladys Knight and the Pips** ("Midnight Train from Georgia") are from Atlanta, and supermodel **RuPaul** lived here for many years. **Blind Willie McTell**, a blues player, lived in Buttermilk Bottoms. **The Indigo Girls** are from nearby Decatur, and rumors constantly crop up speculating that yet another rocker, (fill in the blank), has decided to make Atlanta his or her home.

When the **Sex Pistols** played in Atlanta, they stayed at the Squire Inn, 2115 Piedmont (now a Comfort Inn). Al Kooper, of the Sounds of the South recording studio, an offshoot of MCA, discovered **Lynyrd Skynyrd** in the early 70s. Although they were a group known for drinking and fighting, and were banned from many hotels, Atlanta made the group honorary citizens in 1977. The members of Lynyrd Skynyrd, who recorded "Freebird" and the album, *One More From the Road* live at the Fox, had donated $5,000 to the effort to save the old theatre. Several of them were killed in a plane crash only a few months later.

Stations WSB (the first southern radio station, 1922) and WERD (the first black-owned radio station, 1947) carry on traditions rising out of other parts of the South. WSB stands for **"Welcome South, Brother!" The Royal Peacock** at 186 Auburn has been host to many powerful evenings featuring Cab Calloway, Louis Armstrong, and Aretha Franklin. Jimi Hendrix supposedly met Little Richard (who is from Macon, Georgia) at the Royal Peacock, originally known as the Top

Hat.

Atlanta nurtured the talents of **Mother's Finest**, a black rock and roll funk group from the 70s, as well as the inspiration of RuPaul, supermodel, singer, and actor. **RuPaul and the U-Hauls** (one drag queen plus two large black female singers) entertained at the Nitery (now Eats, on Ponce) in the late 80s.

There are numerous good places to hear music. In Midtown, try **Midtown Music Hall**, in the Highlander Bar (931 Monroe). The **Somber Reptile** with adjacent **Cajun Kitchen**, and **The Wreck Room** cater to the under 25 crowd. These are all next door to one another, on Marietta near Northside Drive (Georgia Tech area and site of the surrender of Atlanta in 1865). **Center Stage** is at Pershing Point (1374 West Peachtree).

**Masquerade**, formerly the Excelsior Mill on North Street (just west of the railroad tracks) arranges itself, Dante fashion, into Heaven, Hell, and Purgatory, with different services on each level. Music can also be found at Little Five Points (Moreland & Euclid) at **The Point**. **Dottie's**, on Memorial Drive just south of Oakland Cemetery, is a good ol' rock and roll honky tonk with pool tables and live bands. **The Scrap Bar**, near Peachtree and 11th, combines welded metal with welded metal. In Buckhead, the **Coca-Cola Roxy** is an old theatre located on Roswell Road, just after it splits from Peachtree. It now features live bands. **"688,"** at 688 Spring Street, right next to the Varsity, was *the* place to see bands in the early 80s. For current listings, consult *Creative Loafing*, a free weekly newspaper available everywhere.

The Sideways pick for the best place to hear music now is the **Clermont Lounge** on Ponce. Strippers pick tunes on the jukebox to strip to.

We'd just as soon stop in at the **Touch of India** to eat great Indian Food and study their collection of autographed photos of politicians and rock stars (is there a difference anymore?) who have dined there while visiting Atlanta. This wonderful restaurant was forced to relocate due to the 1996 Olympics; they plan to reopen at 11th and Peachtree.

Known for the best jukebox is the **Stein Club** (929 Peachtree). Their motto is: "Still straight after all these years." Our favorite juke box place is the **Dunk n' Dine**, at 2277 Cheshire Bridge Road.

The Dunk n' Dine

# Broadview Plaza

The Broadview Plaza (now the Lindbergh Plaza) at the corner of Piedmont and Sidney Marcus Boulevard is the best place in Atlanta to watch sunsets or get Hispanic Videos (**AllStar Video**).

This is also the first place the Sex Pistols played on their ill-fated American tour (in what is now the Office Depot). After the concert, Sid Vicious, wandering around the adjacent neighborhood looking for heroin, missed his flight out of Atlanta. Divine appeared for the opening of John Water's film "Polyester" at the Screening Room.

**The Screening Room** is still a good place to go to see interesting and serious films that never seem to get to the more commercial theatres.

The lucky magnolia tree still stands on the site of
the Georgia Crackers ballfield.


The Dixie Speedway, Woodstock, Georgia

# Chapter 18
# Tomahawkin'

Atlanta is home to the Atlanta Braves, the Atlanta Falcons, the Atlanta Knights, the North Georgia School of Professional Wrestling, and the 1996 Summer Olympics.

It is home to famous golfer **Bobby Jones**, and less famous but equally illustrious golfer **Alexa Stirling**. Miss Stirling in 1915 became the first Atlanta championship golfer, winning the Southern Ladies Golf Women's Championship. For that she was made an honorary member of the (all-male) Capital City Club. Later she went on to win the Womens National in 1916, 1919, and 1920. Both Stirling and Bobby Jones learned to play at the East Lake Golf Club on Glenwood (SE Atlanta). Bobby was only nine when he won his first championship, and in 1930 won all four major world championships. He is buried in Oakland Cemetery with golfballs (left by fans) decorating his grave. Other well-known Atlanta golfers included **Dorothy Kirby**, who won her first trophy at age 13, **Louise Suggs**, who also won four championships in one year (1947), and **Howard Wheeler**, 1938 winner of the Negro National Golf championship.

**Football**, always a fierce rivalry when Georgia Tech and the University of Georgia meet, almost didn't get a toehold in Atlanta after UGA fullback, Richard Von Gammon, died at age 18 from a brain concussion suffered during a Tech-UGA game held at Brisbane Park (Windsor and Glenn Streets). The year was 1897. Horrified, many southern colleges immediately banned football. Atlanta even passed a city anti-football ordinance. The sport was saved finally, by the mother of the victim, who let it be known her son's dying wish (if only he had had one) would have been to save football. Popular opinion rallied around the grieving mother, and football was back before the start of the 1898 season.

Other sports, especially **stock car racing**, have occupied past and present citizens of Atlanta. The track at Paces Ferry was once the fastest half mile in the country. Lakewood Park had a race track (now closed down). In 1947 it was the site of an impromptu high-speed chase when ex-bootlegger Bob Flock, banned from racing at Lakewood, was spotted whipping around the track with other cars. Police gave motorcycle chase, following Bobby through the race, but when two cars collided and the officer saw his chance to make the arrest, Flock took off down the Jonesboro Road at approximately 115 mph. Bobby Flock got away, no problem at all. Today, many other speedways circle Atlanta, but our favorite is the **Dixie Speedway** in Woodstock (north on I-75, then north on I-575). Try to go on a night they feature chain races.

The Atlanta Knights (**Hockey**) won the IHL Turner cup for the 1993-4 season.

**Baseball** is the sport that sits closest to the center of Atlanta's collective soul. Perhaps this is because baseball dates all the way back to when the Creeks won Atlanta from the Cherokee in a series of ballgames held near Standing Peachtree.

The Atlanta Baseball Club was formed in 1866. The first games were played at a park near downtown, and no gloves or mitts were used. In 1884, the first professional baseball games were played. By 1917, a lake at the old Ponce de Leon Park was filled in to make Spiller Field, home of **the Atlanta Crackers** and **the Atlanta Black Crackers**. Across the street, the old springs became Spiller's Fountain of Youth.

The Black Crackers, Negro National Champs in 1938, played at the Spiller Field when the Crackers were out of town. When the Crackers were in town, they would play at Morehouse or Morris Brown College. Exhibition games were often played for fundraising as there was no other backing. The Black Crackers would play the Zulu Giants (men in grass skirts from Florida), or the Cannibals, splitting equally any profit made.

In 1923 the Crackers stadium on Ponce burned down. Injured was "Silver Bill" Stickney, caretaker, asleep in his quarters. A magnolia tree still stands in the back of the stadium. It was good luck to hit a ball into the tree. The last owner of the stadium, Earl Mann, had his ashes scattered under the tree after he died. In 1993, a plaque was dedicated to Mann near the tree, but there is no sign of it now.

In 1926, **Ty Cobb**, in a fundraiser for the Disabled American Veterans, tossed baseballs from the roof of the Hurt Building in downtown Atlanta where they were caught by baseball greats Harry Heilman and Lou Blue. Later the same day, Atlanta played an exhibition game with the Detroit Tigers while the previous Saturday, Babe Ruth hit one right out of the ballpark in a game between the New York Yankees and the Brooklyn Dodgers, held in Atlanta. The Crackers played until 1965, when they were replaced by the Atlanta Braves.

**The Atlanta Braves** were formerly from Milwaukee. Their arrival was celebrated with a replay of that 1926 Yankee/Dodgers game, with the Braves being defeated in their first game by the Pittsburgh Pirates on April 12, 1966. A new stadium had to be built for the new team. The Fulton County Stadium is right downtown, near the intersection of routes 20 and 75/85. Another stadium is being built right next door for the 1996 Summer Olympics, after which the old stadium will be torn down.

Baseball great **Hank Aaron** broke Babe Ruth's record for home runs at the Atlanta-Fulton County Stadium in 1974 with hit #715. He went on to hit 40 more homers before retiring.

In 1976, Ted Turner (CNN), bought the Atlanta Braves, and in 1995, the Braves finally won a World Series.

Atlanta and the Braves touched off a storm of controversy in the early 90s over the issue of **"Tomahawkin'."** Tomahawkin' is an activity involving fans slowly chanting, more or less in unison, a wah-wah-wah Indian war cry and making rhythmic chopping movements with their arms. Done simultaneously by thousands of serious Braves enthusiasts, this simulation is designed to put fear and terror into the hearts of the opposition. It may not surprise some readers to hear that Tomahawkin' is considered to be highly offensive to certain members of the population, notably Native Americans, who maintain that the practice is not only stupid but condescending to their heritage. Demands that sports teams like the Braves, the Redskins, or the Indians switch to some other name has generated great publicity, but affected no change as of yet.

Many Atlantans believe that had the Braves not played the World Series two years in a row in the early 90s, tomahawkin' would never have been seized upon by jealous rivals as something worth criticizing.

# The Parade of Horrors

And you thought this was where we were going to talk about the Olympics!

A gruesome parade of smashed cars and coffins, the sad tolling of a large bell, and the Atlanta Police Band playing "Taps," commemorated the 86 traffic deaths in 1936, during a sad march down Peachtree Street. Every person that died was memorialized by a plaque on one of the 86 coffins draped in black; wrecked cars were splashed with red paint and decorated with tombstones, slogans, and statistics. One man sprawled across the hood of a bashed car to emphasize the result of drinking and driving: "One Killed, Five Injured." The parade was led by the "Four Horsemen of Death."

We were going to resist talking about the 1996 Summer Olympics, but we can't. Three out of our five most favorite restaurants (Thelma's, Cha Gios, and the Touch of India) have been displaced by preparations for the extravaganza and numerous other interesting landmarks and/or buildings have been razed. Call us old sticks-in-the-mud, but couldn't the Olympics have utilized existing resources? This is just a bit more icing on the cake of Atlanta's reputation as a "tear 'em down, build 'em up" kind of city.

We won't even get into the problem of thousands of homeless renters displaced by landlords eager to make an extra buck. And where are all their belongings supposed to be stored when strangers move into their homes and offices??

A revised, improved, post-Olympic edition of *Sideways Atlanta* will reveal the full scope and aftermath of the summer of 1996.

# Chapter 19
## Best Southern Food

**W**e have no desire to attempt to cover all the fabulous restaurants in Atlanta.  Our suggestions for great places to go are based on two main criteria:  1.  They are not expensive; and 2.  They are unique.  So without apologies, we present, simply, the Atlanta restaurants we love the best.

Breakfast in the South, even in a city as sophisticated as Atlanta, still centers around grits.  If you are not a southerner, see the end of this chapter for vital grit information.  Our choice for the best grits served in the city is **Charlie's Sandwich Shop**, downtown behind the old Winecoff Hotel at 10 Ellis Street.  Also located next door to Macys, Charlie's is easily accessible to downtown conventioneers on a budget.

A good breakfast can always be found at the **American Roadhouse** (842 North Highland), but it is crowded on weekends.  We like it for all meals.  In the same neighborhood along Highland are also several other good restaurants.  **Harry and Sons** (Thai, sushi, and pasta), **Surin** (Thai), and **Atkins Park** (a bar) are good stops on your travels.

Our favorite diners are:
**The Silver Skillet**, 200 14th Street: the real 1950s.
**The Majestic**, 1031 Ponce de Leon: 24 hours.
**Dunk n' Dine**, 2277 Cheshire Bridge, near corner of
        Lindbergh.  Great afternoon light, best juke
        box.
**Eats**, 600 Ponce de Leon, just before the Sears
        Building.  Cheap!

**The Varsity** (61 Ponce de Leon) is a unique throwback to days of duck tails and poodle skirts.  A drive-in, you can also walk in to eat.  Bring antacids!  Roll your shirt sleeve around a pack of cigarettes, order a chili dog, and head upstairs to dine in an area reminiscent of an airport. Be sure to get a free hat!

**Eat Your Vegetables** (438 Moreland in Little Five Points) serves lots of veggies with optional meat. It's quieter than many of the other Little Five Point restaurants.

**Savage Pizza** (1250 Virginia Avenue) serves highly imaginative combinations of toppings which include Chinese, Mexican, and Greek; you are free to create your own dream pie.

**Fellini's** has several locations around town. Our favorites are the ones at Little Five Points, Ponce de Leon (923), 1991 Howell Mill Road, and 2813 Peachtree (in Buckhead near the Garden Hills Cinema). Pasta and pizza are glorified here. Fellini's is also known for saving old neon from grocery stores, night clubs, etc. to use for restaurant decoration.

**Frijoleros**, good for burritos, quesadillas, and beer, is located at 11th and Peachtree.

**Tortillas**, at 752 Ponce, is a place to enjoy huge portions while sitting outside on the balcony watching nighthawks swoop and call at dusk.

It's easy to find scores of exciting ethnic restaurants, but again, we present you only with our particular favorites. We are highly subjective!

**Cha Gio's** (Vietnamese) and **Touch of India** have been displaced by the Olympics. These two restaurants are our hands-down favorite ethnic places, so favorite they almost seem to be no longer ethnic, but essential. You would be wise to make the effort to find Cha Gio's new location! Be sure to try their spring and summer rolls. The Touch of India has two locations. One is at the Toco Hills Shopping Center (North Druid Hills and La Vista). The midtown restaurant will relocate to the corner of 11th and Peachtree. Touch of India offers a tasty buffet lunch weekdays. Vegetarian items are available at both establishments.

We are also fond of:

> **La Fonda Latina**, 1159B Euclid (Little Five Points). There is another in Buckhead, with open-air seating, located near the Garden Hills Cinema. Eat the Paella. Vegetarian plates are offered.

> **Bridgetown Grill**, 1156 Euclid (Little Five Points). Try anything with raspberry sauce; Jamaican.

> **The Buford Highway**, no, not the name of a restaurant, but route 13 northeast of the city. The

whole area is Asian; our favorites include Toyota Ya (all you can eat sushi), Pung Mie (Chinese), and Little Szechuan (where the photos of food on the menu look like crime scene photos).

Southern food is its own very special category. We were mourning the demise of our top #1 favorite restaurant, **Thelma's Kitchen**, forced to move from a convenient downtown location to make way for those darned Olympics, when the joyous news spread that Thelma's had reopened at 768 Marietta (near Means). Convenient to both Georgia Tech and the Nexus Contemporary Art Center, Thelma's is reported to be better than ever!

Where else do we go when overwhelmed by cravings for collards, sweet potatoes, Brunswick stew?

**Barbeque Kitchen** (1437 Virginia Avenue, near the airport) offers free refills--of vegetables. Across the street is the College Park Cemetery where stripper Chili Evans is buried.

The **Beautiful Restaurant** (397 Auburn, corner of Jackson) is right next door to the Ebenezer Baptist Church, serving all our favorite southern foods.

**Soul Vegetarian I & II** (Highland Avenue, 1 block south of Ponce, or 879 Ralph D. Abernathy, near Ashby) are also good choices for *essential* southern nutrition.

We have very bad taste in snacks. Our favorite is **Krispy Kreme** (motto: "Hot Donuts Now!") at 295 Ponce. Watching the donut army marching bravely into great vats of fat is second only to watching the wide variety of other humanoids frequenting the establishment, especially late in the evening. Nearby **Zesto's**, at 544 Ponce, is the place to go for malted milk shakes.

---

## Our top 5 favorite restaurants:

*Thelmas*
*Cha Gio's*
*Touch of India*
*Savage Pizza*
*Eats*

---

The **DeKalb Farmer's Market**, 3000 E. Ponce de Leon in Decatur, not ony offers a mind-boggling selection of seafood, meat, and produce from all over the world, it also boasts a cafeteria featuring delicious and generous portions of ethnic and southern food.

Out of town, a pilgrimage to the **Big Chicken** (a Kentucky Fried Chicken in Marietta) is required. After the 56 foot giant chicken statue was damaged, Atlantans were asked to vote on the restoration--the original chicken or a more "modern" one. Both versions had charming moving eyes, but the traditional chicken won and restoration began in 1993. Stop in at Cobb County's Big Chicken the day you drop by Speaker Newt's home office in Morrow at 6351 Jonesboro Road. Call first to see if he wants some chicken: 968-3219.

For dessert, we must confess to leaning toward those hot donuts. If we're in a classy mood, however, we head to **Cafe Diem**, one block south of Ponce on Highland. Fab pastries in a european cafe atmosphere is a little heavy for us; we get the goodies to go. For coffee, especially in the morning, it's the **San Francisco Coffee Roasting Company** at 1192 N. Highland Avenue. Besides serving the most full-bodied (strong!) coffee in Atlanta, the scones are to die for. For plain old regular straight coffee, **Dunk n' Dine** is our place to go.

We have eaten at scores of other fine restaurants, even, on occasion, more expensive ones! The places mentioned here, though, are the ones we return to again and again, and again. We hope you'll try some of our suggestions, and we're sure you'll agree!

The Big Chicken being rebuilt

# Grits

Grits are a uniquely southern food. Made from grinding corn, corn is the product; the gritty by-product is grits. Cornmeal and grits form a cornerstone of essential food staples in the south.

No one seems to agree whether grits is singular or if grits are plural.

Southerners love grits. Almost no one else has ever heard of them. Craig Claiborne, a southerner and New York Times food editor, has a recipe for grits souffle. Grits are sometimes cooked with garlic and jalapenos for a southwestern twang. Most real sons of the south eat grits for breakfast and grits is what you will get with your order unless you say otherwise.

The correct cooking of grits is an artform. They look a bit like large-grained cream of wheat but are eaten with butter, salt, and pepper. Wipe them up with your toast. Do not commit the Yankee faux-pas of ordering them with milk and sugar. Try the grits at Charlie's, downtown near the corner of Ellis and Peachtree. Bill Tomey says they're the best in town! However, Bill also says, "Grits are *not* bland. They should taste like Cream of Wheat!"

For all the information you ever wanted to know about grits, and much, much more, see *Grits*, a 1988 film documentary by Stan Woodward.

# Chapter 20
# West End & Beyond

Centered around the West End, the West Side of Atlanta stretches from I-75/85 to the Chattahoochee River or I-285, whichever comes first. Included in this area is Standing Peachtree, the original Atlanta settlement.

After Atlanta was established in its present location (centering around the Zero Mile Marker near Five Points), the spread of life and commerce to the west included notorious Snake Nation (Peters & Castelberry) with Happy Hollow nearby, and Elbow Bend (at Haynes & Markham). These neighborhoods were located just below what is now the Georgia Dome and World Congress Center, west of Five Points.

**The White Hall Tavern**, on the east side of Lee between Gordon and Park, was right in the middle of what is now the West End neighborhood. The tavern, built by Charner Humphries in 1835, was a center of activity with a U.S. Post Office, a stagecoach stop, and the local militia, who met and practiced here. It was supposedly burned at the close of the Civil War (there are varying accounts), and it was never rebuilt. Humphries and his family are buried at Westview Cemetery.

**Atlanta's West End**, a designated Historic District, centers around Ashby and Ralph D. Abernathy Boulevard (RDA). RDA is the former Gordon Street. The West End community boasts many homes built during the Victorian era, now being restored. The area is recovering from economic deterioration experienced in the 1960s and 70s with the help of influence from a strong African-American and Muslim community.

**The Wren's Nest** is located here (1050 RDA), home of Joel Chandler Harris and his pals B'rer Rabbitt and B'rer Fox (see Chapter 21). Right around the corner at 503 Peeples Street lived Madge Bingham, author of many children's books. Her house is now the **Hammonds House**, a gallery and resource center for African-American Art. In this neighborhood is also located the **Shrine of the Black Madonna Culture Center**, 946 RDA (752-6125) and the **Soul Vegetarian Restaurant** (just east of Ashby on RDA).

Head north on Ashby to visit **Atlanta's six historic Black colleges**: Spellman College, Atlantic University, Morehouse College, Clark College, Atlanta University, and Morris Brown College. The first, Atlanta University, was chartered in 1867, right after the Civil War. These institutions have established a setpoint for African-American culture and learning, boasting many important graduates. The colleges also play host to the yearly Atlanta nightmare, **"Freaknik,"** a sort of urban spring break for tens of thousands of black college students.

The home of Alonzo Herndon, born a slave, founder of the Atlanta Life Insurance Company, is nearby at 587 University Place. **The Herndon Home**, an important historic center, schedules tours every hour. Call 581-9813 for information.

On the south side of Atlanta University, in the old neighborhood of Beaver Slide, one of Atlanta's first public housing projects was built in 1933, University Homes. The other project, Techwood, below Georgia Tech, was built the same year.

Return to Martin Luther King, Jr. Drive (MLK).

Drive west to the **Washington Park** area, a neighborhood working to establish status as a Historic District. The park itself (turn right on Ashby and left on Desoto), was Atlanta's first black public park. Nearby (Ashby & Booker) is Booker T. Washington High School, the first black public high school in Atlanta.

Continue driving west on MLK. Just after you pass under I-20, turn right on Anderson, left on Penelope Road, and right on Penelope Drive to 1817, **former home of Wayne Williams**, 23-year-old photographer connected with the killings of 28 young African-Americans in the early 80s. Williams was actually convicted of murdering only two.

South of **Westview Cemetery** is the area where the **"Lover's Lane Killings"** took place in 1977. Two incidents in Adams Park (south of Greenwood Cemetery and Cascade Road) and one at West Manor Park (near the intersection of Lynhurst and Benjamin E. Mays Drive), are still unsolved. The killer has not struck again, as far as anyone knows, but we still recommend going somewhere else for your necking activities.

From Benjamin Mays, heading back toward Atlanta, turn left on Peyton Road and go north to MLK, jog right and left on route 280 (Hightower Road). Stay on 280; it becomes James Jackson Parkway. You will see the **Pet Cemetery** on the left just before crossing Proctor Creek.  Continue north to the Chattahoochee River.  This bridge is where Wayne Williams was seen dropping something in the middle of the night of May 22, 1981.  It turned out to be the body of Nathaniel Cater, who was found downstream near the I-285 bridge.

**The Chattahoochee River**, not usually littered with dead bodies, is more often populated with kayakers and fly fishermen.  "The Chat" is a river park, 48 miles long, beginning near the intersection of I-75 and I-285.  The park is a very good place to go to escape the heat on a hot summer day. Stop in at the southernmost information center off Cobb Parkway (route 41) for hints on places to go.  The park information number is 394-8335. When in the park, watch out for the abundant poison ivy!

Double-decker bus graveyard where
Brad Pitt (as Early Grace) buried his landlord
in *Kalifornia* (see page 121)

# Elephant Tears

Atlanta was touched by a particularly sad tragedy in November 1941. The Ringling Brothers-Barnum & Bailey Circus was in town, normally a wonderful event. Instead, a clown, an accountant, and eight elephants died sudden, mysterious deaths. After the circus left town, two more elephants died, bringing the total deaths to twelve. Suspected cause was deliberate poisoning of the water with arsenic. It turned out the men died of heart attacks, but the mass murderer of Alice, Little Lizzie, Ringling's Lizzie, Clara, Blanche, Tilly, Mary, Mable, Puqua, and Palms (a baby) was never apprehended. Of the animals who got sick, only one, Peggy, survived. The elephants are buried in a mass grave near Howell Station.

Take Northside Drive (route 3) north to West Marietta and go left. At Marietta and Brady (on the right) are the former **National Stockyards**, at one time the largest mule market in the country. At Brady and Howell Mill was the **Peach Bowl Speedway**, once hosting Lady Lion Tamer turned Stock Car Racer Miss Ann Wesley. The **elephants are buried** a little further up the road. As near as we can tell (reports were vague), the burial took place on the other side of the railroad tracks along the north side of West Marietta, between Ashby and Herndon. There is no marker.

Go right at the first big intersection, Marietta Boulevard. At Huff Road, turn right again. At the southeast corner of Marietta and Huff was **"The House of Three Flags."** The house was saved from destruction by raising the Confederate flag when that army used the house as headquarters, by raising the Union flag when the Yankees also used the house for headquarters, and with a British flag when Sherman set fire to Atlanta.

Continue to Foster Street. The **Atlanta Water Works** is on your left; Foster is on the right. The entrance to Foster Street is usually decorated with works of art; you are entering an artists' community. Go down Foster and take a right on the dirt road to see the place where **Brad Pitt**, as Early Grace in the film *Kalifornia* killed his landlord and buried him. Near the **double-decker bus graveyard**, look back from where you came to see the scene.

Back on Huff, go to Howell Mill Road and turn left, then right on Bishop. Between Howell Mill and Northside Drive (which intersects Bishop), you can get a great view of the skyline with the Georgia Dome to the right looking like Gamera coming to destroy Atlanta.

Nearby **Maria's Restaurant** at 1330 Northside Drive (corner of Bishop) is where Early Grace's girlfriend (Juliette Lewis) stole a cactus from the cigarette machine (and named it "Shelley"). Behind Maria's is a fenced-in flag dedicated to **Alvin B. Avery**, a worker who was electrocuted at the Water Works in 1989.

# Chapter 21
# The Wren's Nest

**N**ot to be missed by any serious Atlantophile is Joel Chandler Harris's home, the Wren's Nest. Harris is best known for the Br'er Rabbit stories, a series of African-American folk tales based on animal friends and told by their translator, Uncle Remus. Harris, who was also a journalist for the *Atlanta Constitution*, wrote the stories to try to introduce an atmosphere of healing after the War Between the States. The stories, serialized in newspapers. were first published in book form in 1880. Throughout his lifetime, Harris wrote over 30 books, including the Uncle Remus stories. Born and raised in Eatonton, Georgia, Harris is buried in West View Cemetery.

The Wren's Nest, located in Atlanta's West End at 1050 Ralph D. Abernathy Boulevard, is a National Historic Landmark. Originally built in 1867, the house is an interesting example of the "dogtrot" pattern of architecture, one which centers on a wide, middle hallway with rooms on either side to facilitate efficient (cooling) air circulation during the hot summer months. In 1884, a Queen Anne Victorian style facade was installed during a renovation that also greatly enlarged the size of the house. The Harris family lived there until 1913, when Mrs. Harris sold it to the Uncle Remus Memorial Association.

Guided tours are available of this wonderful house, which is still in the process of being restored. The visitor will see many of the original furnishings, including bookcases with copies of Harris's books which, unfortunately, you are not allowed to look through. When you walk around the house, it really seems as if the Harris family is still there, maybe right in the next room. African-Americans were not admitted here until 1968.

There is a small museum shop selling, among other things, copies of some of the more popular Uncle Remus stories and anthologies. Much of this stuff was mutated (or, some would say, updated) by the Disney production *Song of the South*, and if the shop might jar you out of your reverie of days gone by, do not despair. Continue right on out the back door and into the shady back yard and wait, for hours if necessary, for Storyteller Akbar Imhotep to bring Br'er Rabbit's adventures back to life. Mr. Imhotep is a truly gifted storyteller, and if you sit for awhile in the grove of trees in the backyard of the Wren's Nest while he speaks, listening to the birds and enjoying the cool breezes, you might suddenly see Br'er Rabbit jumping out from behind a bush, and Br'er Fox giving him chase. On a lovely summer's afternoon, this is a transcendental experience.

Call 753-7735 before you plan to go, and make sure the storyteller will be sitting out back, waiting for you! You can get to the Wren's Nest via MARTA (West End stop) and by then taking bus #S-2. By car, take I-20 west to the Ashby exit, go south on Ashby, and right on Ralph D. Abernathy Boulevard. It's about two blocks, on your left. A good nearby restaurant to visit is the Soul Vegetarian, at 879 RDA, just on the other side of Ashby. Call 752-5194 for hours and specials.

The Wren's Nest

# Chapter 22
# Buckhead

**W**e don't have much use for Buckhead. Spread between Interstates 75 and 85, it begins roughly where the two routes come together and ends . . . well, who knows exactly where it all ends? Buckhead is a mecca for the rich and glittery, and for the rich and glittery wannabes. It is a good place to observe the effects of an excess of conspicuous consumption. Shoppers congregate in such large numbers around Lenox Square and Phipps Plaza (malls across the street from one another), they create traffic hazards in an already congested area. Shopping bliss was disturbed in 1977 with the arrival of George Mitchell, a 28-year-old **footstomper**. Mitchell accosted women at both Lenox Square and Phipps Plaza by either simply stomping on their feet, or by dropping cans of food on their feet. While doing this, he would stare the woman right in the eyes. Previously arrested in Nashville for similar offenses, he was arrested on twelve counts of simple battery in Atlanta, mostly for broken toes.

If you still want to go to Buckhead, take Peachtree Street out of downtown and through midtown. Once you cross I-85, you are in Buckhead. Eventually Peachtree branches into Roswell and Peachtree Roads; follow Peachtree Road to the malls and beyond.

The lower section of Buckhead presents many areas of interest. **Tula**, on the left just past Piedmont Hospital, is an arts complex housing prestigious galleries, shops, and artists' studios. Several blocks north and on the left will be Peachtree Battle Avenue, site of the **Civil War Battle of Peachtree Creek**. Right across the street is a shopping center we often frequent for Oxford Books, Oxford Too, and a good laundromat. **Oxford Books** has a good coffeeshop inside and is supposedly the place to go in the evening to look for dates!

The **Garden Hills Cinema**, opening in 1939 at 2835

Peachtree is one of three theatres in Atlanta showing films of real substance.

The place where Peachtree forks is significant. The earliest Buckhead establishment, the **Buckhead Tavern**, was located here. Another **Oxford Bookstore** is located on Pharr Road about three blocks east of Peachtree. This bookstore, once an auto dealership, also has a coffeeshop inside.

At the fork, go straight ahead on Roswell to see the **Cotton Exchange Building** (3155 on the right, one block north of the fork) where Klan robes were once manufactured. You are right across the street from the **Rib Shack**, a good, shady, and congenial place to stop by and have a snack.

Turn left on West Paces Ferry Road (where Peachtree splits) to visit the **Atlanta History Center**, headquarters for all things Atlanta (except *Sideways Atlanta*). A new museum has recently opened, adding outstanding exhibitions to the other facilities: the 1840 Tullie Smith House, the 1928 Swan House mansion, the Library Archives, and the Cherokee Garden Library.

The Library Archives, where our hero, Franklin M. Garrett still holds court, contains books, personal papers, more than 1,000,000 photos, and an important section for geneological researchers. A treasure trove of information, the archive is open to the public. Early mornings are mostly uncrowded, and are the best times to get help from a very friendly and accommodating staff. The Cherokee Garden Library, also open to the public, features rare books on gardening as well as material on historic to contemporary and all aspects of horticulture with emphasis on the south.

To see all the Atlanta History Center has to offer (and without doing any research), allow at least half as day. Call 814-4000 for information and hours. And don't forget the branch office downtown!

Drive west on West Paces Ferry to see huge elaborate homes, including the governor's mansion (on the right just past Woodhaven Road). Continue west, and if you're all pumped up from your visit to the History Center, go left at the fork (Moore's Mill Road) and head for Standing Peachtree (see chapters 1&2).

# The Debs

**W**hat could be more southern than the vision of a beautiful young lady, flanked by two escorts, being formally introduced to genteel society at a sumptuous ball?

Debutantes.

According to our secret source, brother of a modern-day deb, the formal introduction is the culmination of a year-long series of teas, luncheons, and parties designed to teach the 17 and 18-year-olds about society, their responsibilities, and their privileges.

Sixty-nine girls each year are chosen to be debutantes by either the Atlanta Debutante Club or the Phoenix Club, in a series of appointments and luncheons with the girl and her mother. After their selection, the girls meet as a group. Then, each girl, with her mother, in a game of one-upmanship, plans a theme event such as a "Lace Luncheon," a "Riverboat Party" with Huck Finn attire, or maybe a "Champagne Tea Dance." At some point, wearing white eyelet, the girls celebrate their coming out with a ribbon dance around a maypole. A gift for both the hostess and her mother must be brought by each guest to each soiree. Finally, around Christmas, the main event is held at the Piedmont Driving Club.

During their busy year, debs are also expected to perform community service by working in hospitals, nursing homes, or participating in various fundraising events. Once the shock of coming out (and paying for it) wears off, these young society ladies turn their efforts to good deeds through the Junior League and other important volunteer activities.

The object of debhood? Matrimony.

*Sideways Atlanta* will continue their investigation into this highly secretive cult activity.

# Atlanta's Most Ironic Places

**Standing Peachtree:** now a Waste Water plant

**Humbug Square:** now Underground Atlanta

**Robert Crawford's Slave Yards** at #10 Peachtree Street: now a Fashion & Gift Mart

**Red Light District** at Decatur & Courtland: now the flashing red light display of the World of Coca-Cola

**World of Sid & Marty Krofft,** puppeteers & vaudevillians: now home of CNN

Site where General William Tecumseh Sherman watched **The Battle of Atlanta:** now the Jimmy Carter Presidential Center

**Cobb County** (Newt Gingrich's district):  #11 in college education and #25 in median income nationwide, #3 in federal subsidies received

**The Wren's Nest,** home of the author of the African-American B'rer Rabbit and B'rer Fox folktales: didn't admit blacks until 1968

# Chapter 23
# Arts Tour

**M**any out-of-towners will be surprised to hear of Atlanta's active, vibrant art scene. Artists working in the city are delighted to find not only are they able to find places to show their work, but it actually sells too! One possible reason for this is that Atlanta is a city with money (see Buckhead) and is also a Southeastern regional center for culture, drawing in art lovers from outlying areas. Big exception: Cobb County (see chapter 26).

We did not find much information on interesting artists working before 1900. Mention is made of a **Mrs. L. Condon**, artist and photographer, supposedly the only lady photographer in the South. She came to Atlanta in 1890 from Louisville, and worked at 83 Whitehall Street. Beginning in the twenties, artists congregated around the Baltimore Block (Midtown), but gradually they spread throughout the city until there was no specific place to find them.

Atlanta's art scene took a heavy blow in 1962 when 106 members of the Atlanta Art Association, on an art-cultural tour of Europe, died in a **plane crash in Paris**. A Rodin sculpture, a gift from France, memorializes the tragedy. It is located at the Woodruff Arts Center, which was built as a remembrance to that art community. The **High Museum of Art** at the Woodruff Arts Center (just north of 14th and Peachtree) presents a combination of contemporary and traditional art in both permanent and changing exhibitions. Call 892-HIGH. Adjacent is the **Atlanta College of Art**, which also exhibits the work of students, faculty, alumni, and hosts various themed shows. Call 898-1157 for information. The High Museum recently opened a branch at the **Georgia Pacific Center** downtown. This interesting space is devoted mainly to Photography and the Folk Arts.

Emory University (off Decatur Road in northeast Atlanta) offers the **Michael C. Carlos Museum** which emphasises

Ancient Art from all cultures. Call 727-4282.

The **Hammonds House** in the West End (503 Peeples Street, 752-8730) is a resource center and exhibition space for African American Art. The **Nexus Contemporary Art Center** (535 Means Street, off Techwood Parkway, 688-2500) boasts a huge exhibition space for contemporary and multi-disciplinary art. The internationally significant Nexus Press specializes in limited edition artist books and book arts.

The **TULA** complex in Buckhead (75 Bennett Street) hosts the renowned **Lowe Gallery**, directed by the charming Bill Lowe and his enthusiastic staff. The space is very large, encouraging the exhibition of monumental sculpture and painting. (Call 352-8114). Smaller galleries in TULA include the **Galerie Timothy Tew** (352-0665) which consistently presents provocative contemporary art in an intimate space. A Photography Gallery and an Artists' Co-op are among the other ventures represented there; a number of artists and photographers also keep studios in the complex.

Photography galleries include **Fay Gold** (247 Buckhead Avenue, 233-3843) and **Jackson Fine Art** (515 E. Paces Ferry, 233-3739).

The **Callanwolde Fine Arts Center**, a lovely estate in Druid Hills (980 Briarcliff Road, 872-5338), exhibits work by local artists. They also host many worthwhile art programs, including performing arts, poetry, and storytelling.

Many alternative spaces provide an essential counterpoint to the mainstream activities. In addition to Nexus, **The Arts Exchange Gallery** (750 Kalb Street, 624-4211), located adjacent to the Atlanta Stockade, houses artist studios. A gallery benefitting persons with HIV/AIDS, **Koolhipfunkystuff**, at 1030 Monroe near Virginia (607-1095), is in an area peppered with other fine galleries.

The **Atlanta Gallery Association** publishes a complete gallery guide, available free at many of the places listed here.

Atlanta has hosted the annual **Arts Festival of Atlanta** for more than 40 years. A week-long event, the festival features both performing and visual arts, and work by artists from across the country. A prospectus mailed out almost a year in advance details the juried competitions for public sculpture, billboard art, city bus posters, and postcards in addition to special gallery exhibition all over the city. The Festival, centered in Piedmont Park, includes a great arts & crafts fair. For more information, call 885-1125. The Festival is usually held in September.

# Chapter 25
# Daily Life

There's nothing worse than wandering around in a strange city wondering where to do laundry, get groceries, get gas, or, worst of all, to find a car mechanic. We hope our suggestions will help you feel more at home in Atlanta. We also hope you will ask Atlantans for advice. Be brave! People everywhere are usually friendly and willing to help. Travelers tend to assume locals everywhere are constantly busy preparing unpleasant surprises for unsuspecting tourists.

A word about conversations with southerners: don't talk so much (especially if you're a Yankee!), and listen more. You'll usually get your information plus a good story or two! The tendency of southerners to tell long stories is not a myth. Visitors are honored if they are able to come home with one or two good stories under their belts!

Especially good places everywhere to get information and advice are hardware stores and barber shops. Libraries come in a distant third!

Here in Atlanta, we have prepared a sampling of some of our favorite places to go for these essential services:

**Coffee**
> The San Francisco Coffee Company, 2 locations at 1192
> North Highland or 4200 Paces Ferry Road.
> Very trendy, great scones!

> The Dunk n' Dine, near the corner of Cheshire Bridge and
> Lindbergh.

**Groceries**
> DeKalb Farmers Market, 3000 E. Ponce de Leon, Decatur.
> The size of two football fields with mind-boggling
> choices.

Sevenanda, 1111 Euclid Ave in Little Five Points. Natural foods, community-owned.

Harris Teeter, 6111 Peachtree-Dunwoody Road, across from the Brookhaven MARTA station and Druid Hills Road. Very upscale grocery store, many exotic and elegant foods prepared on the premises.

## Barbershops

Healy Building, 57 Forsyth Street (Downtown). Great atrium, and Bill's favorite shop.

Wild Bill's Cherokee Barbershop, 10th Street, near Howell Mill. See many unique decorations, including a photo of the just-hanged Leo Frank.

## Laundry

Star Wash, Peachtree Battle Shopping Plaza, Peachtree & Peachtree Battle. Visit Oxford Books while waiting.

Laundry Lounge, Ansley Mall, corner of Monroe & Piedmont. Many services in this mall, including Morrison's Cafeteria.

## Bookstores

Oxford at Peachtree Battle Shopping Plaza (2345 Peachtree). Check out Oxford Too for comics, used, remaindered, rare, and regional books.

Oxford at 360 Pharr Rd (near the Atlanta History Center).

## Movies

Garden Hills Cinema, 2835 Peachtree, 266-2202.
Plaza Theatre, 1049 Ponce de Leon, 873-1939.
Screening Room, Broadview Plaza, 231-1924.

## Drive-Ins

Starlight Six Drive-In Theatre, 2000 Moreland, 627-5786.
North 85 Twin Drive-In Theatre, 3265 Northeast Expressway Access Road, Chamblee, 451-4570.

## Copying

Kinko's (many locations):
Downtown, 1 Park Place South.
Midtown, 793 Peachtree Street.
Emory, 1385 Oxford Road.

## Photo Processing

Camera Bug, 1799 Briarcliff Road, Sage Hill Plaza.
One hour processing.

Crown Camera, 1000 Piedmont (at 10th).

## Gas & Car Repair

My Favorite Mechanic, Inc. is a Woman, Little Five Points,
1618 DeKalb between Clifton and Moreland, 371-
9912.

Pete Levine's Auto Repair, 1916 Piedmont Circle, 875-
7212 in the (Monroe, Cheshire Bridge, Piedmont area).
Good antique toys in the waiting room; Bill's favorite.

Emory Chevron, 1574 North Decatur Road, 373-7400.
Jimmy & Carolyn, proprietors; Suzanne's favorite.

Sonny's Auto Service, 4525 Glenwood Road, Decatur,
284-6488. Near the DeKalb Farmer's Market, have
your car fixed by Sonny and Bubba; Aunt Sandra's
favorite.

## MARTA

The city train/bus system allows you to park outside town
and ride in. Good places to park are the Avondale station in
Decatur, the Lindbergh station, and the Brookhaven station.
Visitor passes (2-5 days) are available, as are monthly passes.

## Vets and Kennels

Northside Pet Hospital and Buckhead Pet Hotel, 1634 Northside Drive near I-75. 350-9827.

Sugarloaf Pet Resort, 14365 Cogburn Road, Alpharetta. 475-9220. Expensive but excellent care in a country setting. Nightly Frosty Paws parties!

## Radio Stations

| | | |
|---|---|---|
| WGST | 640 AM | News. |
| WREK | 91.9 FM | Eclectic, Georgia Tech station. |
| WKLS | 96 ROCK | Rock and roll from mid-70s on. |
| WRFG | 89.3 FM | Blues, bluegrass, classic country. |
| WABE | 90 FM | Classical, Public Radio. |
| KICKS | 101.5 FM | Current country. |
| WNNX | 99X | Mainstream alternative. |

Big Guitar Player, near Conyers

# Chapter 25
# Out of Town Trips

**W**e've grouped tours together by locale; a variety of different kinds of sights to see is our favorite way to roadtrip. Interstates are the easiest way to get out of town, but we recommend you get off and take back roads as quickly as possible to get a better taste of rural Georgia and the South.

### Tour #1: the Southeast Region
Drive east on I-20 to Madison. Take route 441 south to the Rock Eagle 4-H Center to see a giant rock eagle with a 120 foot wingspan. The origin is a mystery, but it is manmade. Stay on 441 to Eatonton, birthplace of Joel Chandler Harris, to see the large statue of Br'er Rabbit in the town square. Continue south to Milledgeville, home of the State Insane Asylum where Julia Force spent her life after killing her two sisters. Go west on route 49 to Macon, birthplace of Little Richard and Capricorn Records. Duane Allman and Berry Oakley, both of the Allman Brothers Band, are buried in Macon's Rose Hill Cemetery. Head north on route 16 and then on route 23 to Juliette, town where the film *Fried Green Tomatoes* was made in 1991. Fried green tomatoes are available. Return to Atlanta via I-75.

### Tour #2: the Southern Region
Drive south on I-75 to route 26 (Henderson). Go west to Andersonville, where during the Civil War Federal soldiers were held prisoner. The Andersonville Confederate Prison Site and Andersonville National Cemetery are here, as well as a Civil War museum. Drive southwest on route 49 to Plains (21 miles), home of former President Jimmy Carter. The Plains Railroad Depot has a museum dedicated to Carter. Return to Americus, and drive north on route 30 to Buena Vista. Turn north on route 137 to see "Pasaquan." Now owned by the Marion County Historical Society, the house

and surroundings were created by folk artist/bartender/fortuneteller Eddie O. Martin (Saint EOM).  Using concrete and house paint, Martin, who often dressed in large feather headdresses, built furniture, shrines, totem poles, and pagodas into his home.  His work continued from 1957 until his death in 1986.  Call 912-649-9444 for more information on the artist and visiting hours .

It is but a short jaunt from here to tour #3; drive it backwards if you are coming from tour #2.

**Tour #3: the Southwest Region**

Take I-75/85 south to I-85 to route 29 (exit 8) to Moreland.  See the restoration efforts being made on behalf of "The Little Manse," boyhood home of author Erskine Caldwell.  Call 675-6721 for information.  Caldwell was an important writer on conditions of the south during the Depression.  Take alt. 27 south to Manchester to see the Magic Magnetic Hill where autos roll uphill and won't coast downhill.  Optical illusions?  We scoff at unbelievers!  Head west to Warm Springs, President Franklin D. Roosevelt's retreat, and then to Callaway Gardens, 12,000 acres of golf, fishing, and other sports.  The gardens themselves are extensive and impressive, and include a unique butterfly center.  Summer activities revolve around water ski shows and operas, to name two.  Hotel facilities include "villas" and cottages; dining ranges from casual to elegant.  Callaway is a good place to visit just for a day, or to spend a few days in luxurious relaxation.  The Callaway Gardens are located in Pine Mountain off highway 27.  Call 800-282-8181 for information, reservations, and prices.

**Tour #4: the Western Region**

From Atlanta, take route 78 west to Austell, site of the 1958 capture of the Rhesus monkey posing as a space alien.  Continue west on 78 to Villa Rica, where the lavish "Gone With the Wind" theme park is planned.  Drive south on route 61 to Carrollton, where actress Susan Hayward is buried.

Tours #1-4 could be hooked together, in that order.  At least three days should be allowed, especially if you want to spend any substantial time at Andersonville, Plains, Warm Springs, or Callaway Gardens.

## Tour #5: a Folk Art Tour

Summerville, Georgia is the home of the Reverend Howard Finster and his garden of art and religious narrative. Although the Reverend is very well-known to the art world, the artwork still maintains his original spirit. Take I-75 north to Adairsville, go east on route 140 and north on route 27 to Summersville. North of town, turn right on Rena Street.

The Pig Hill of Fame, on route 515 in East Ellijay, boasts more than 1,300 plywood pigs on the hillside above Poole's Barbeque. Do they add a pig everytime a real one is cooked? Leave Summerville going south, take route 156 east to route 411 north, then route 76 east to Ellijay.

## Tour #6: Chattanooga, the favorite tour of your authors

Head straight up I-75 to reverse Sherman's march through Georgia and visit one of our most well-loved places, Fairyland Caverns, located in the wonderful and unique Rock City. Built in 1932, Rock City covers 14 acres of both natural and decorated rocks in a kind of "lawn art gone beserk" motif. Swinging bridges create irresistible urges to jump up and down on them, especially if there is a group of debutantes on board! To get to Rock City, go west on route 24 (in Chattanooga). Take exit 178 and follow highway 58. Look for the many Rock City signs.

Backtrack a bit and drive north on route 148 to find the Ruby Falls Caverns and a good cave tour. We are particularly fond of caves, and try to include at least one on every road-trip. Nearby you will also find the quintessentially southern "Confederama" (re-named the "Battle of Chattanooga") and the very scary incline railroad that takes you to the top of Lookout Mountain. Be sure to sit in the front seat for the most frightening effect. The top of Lookout Mountain gives a good view of the curving river below and a great appreciation of the loyalty and dedication Civil War soldiers must have had to drag their heavy artillery up what looks like an almost vertical incline, only to risk death at the top!

Do not return to Atlanta without stopping at Ringgold (just south of Chattanooga) where, if in the mood, you and your beloved need wait only three hours to get married. George Jones and Tammy Wynette did, on February 16, 1969.

## Tour #7: the North Georgia Mountains

The mountains are a good place to go when the heat and/or general city congestion becomes unbearable. Take I-75 to I-285 (the loop around Atlanta) to route 19 north.

Dahlonega (Dah-lon'-eh-gah) was once the center of gold mining activity in Georgia; there are still places you can pan for gold. A gold mining museum is here, along with many shops. West of Dahlonega is Amicalola Falls, start of the Appalachian Trail. Walk a few feet on it so you can tell your friends you walked the trail!

Raybun County, northeast of Dahlonega, centers around the town of Clayton (routes 76 and 23/441). This is the area where the classic film *Deliverance* was made.

Drive south on route 441 to Cornelia, and stay at Joni Mabe's Elvis Bed and Breakfast. Cornelia is also home of "The Big Apple." The next day, travel south to Gainesville to see R.A. Miller's yard of whirligigs on route 13 outside of town. Just east of Gainesville is Rabbittown, with its own "Big Rabbitt" statue. Travel east on route 129 to Jefferson, birthplace of anesthesia and home of the Crawford W. Long Museum. Exhibits cover the history of anesthesia, including a diorama of the first operation using anesthesia. The Jackson County Historical Society is also in the museum, located at 28 College Street, 706-367-5307. Jefferson is five miles off I-85 at exit 50.

Go north on route 15 to Commerce, home of Olive Ann Burns, author of *Cold Sassy Tree*, a novel and movie based on the town of Commerce.

A little out of the way is Elberton and the Georgia Guidestones. Engraved on this 20-foot rock monument are bits of wisdom and philosophy in many languages. Built only about ten years ago, they were commissioned and paid for by a stranger, who then disappeared. Find the stones on route 77 north of Elberton. Continue north on route 77 to Hartwell, the only county and town named for a woman, Nancy Hart. Living in the area during the Revolutionary War, Hart's house was occupied by Tories who demanded food. She cooked them an old turkey, slipping their guns to her husband through cracks in the wall. When caught, she grabbed a gun, threatened to shoot, and did. The rest of the Tories were captured and hung in the woods at Nancy Hart Spring. Many other stories are told about this large and powerful woman. She was feared and respected by everyone. Nancy Hart State Park off route 29, houses a reproduction of her cabin. The Indians named War Woman Creek in her honor.

**Tour #8: Conyers**

Head for Conyers on the 13th of every month for your chance to see or hear the Blessed Virgin Mary.

## Tour #9: Stone Mountain

Also known as Rock Mountain and New Gibralter, the Stone Mountain monolith of granite rises out of the earth to a height of 825 feet. Seen from a distance, especially from the air, it looks quite a bit like Australia's Ayers Rock . . . but with the giant figures of three Confederate Generals carved onto the north face. Surrounded by Stone Mountain Park, the area is a good place to go for R&R. In addition to the sculpture, visitors can ride a skylift to the top or a train around the bottom, enjoy many wildlife and nature trails, and see a Southern Plantation, consisting of almost two dozen restored buildings moved from other parts of Georgia. One of the slave cabins is the old Medicine House of Dr. Chapman Powell, built in 1833 and originally located at the corner of Clairmont and North Decatur.

The first structure built on top of Stone Mountain was Cloud's Tower. Erected in 1839, it was a 165-foot wooden pyramid with 300 steps. Dances were held in the lower hall.

The mountain has a notorious past. On Thanksgiving night, 1915, the Ku Klux Klan was resurrected in a ceremony on the top of Stone Mountain. The original Klan had died out after the Reconstruction; the new Klan, legally chartered by the State of Georgia, was destined to sweep the country. For many years, crosses were burned at the top of Stone Mountain, and could be seen for miles.

Stone Mountain is 16 miles east of Atlanta on highway 78. Take Ponce de Leon Avenue to route 8 (Scott Boulevard), which runs into Lawrenceville Highway, which runs into Stone Mountain Parkway. For less congestion, take I-20 east to I-285 north to I-78 east (Stone Mountain Parkway). Public transportation is available through the MARTA system; call for information.

## Tour #10: Cobb County

Cobb County has thrust itself into the consciousness of the country recently both with its 1994 anti-gay resolution and with the ascendance of 6th district Congressman Newt Gingrich.

The resolution, ultimately resulting in Cobb County losing its venue for Olympic volleyball, cut off all arts subsidies to the county. Despite very bad national publicity the resolution has not been rescinded.

Former Governor Lester Maddox, age 80 and still occasionally riding his bike backwards in local parades, lives in Marietta. Kennesaw State College is home to Newt's controversial televised classes/infomercials.

For all its conservative facade, Cobb County, nationally ranked #11 in college degrees (40%) and #25 in median income ($47,000), is #3 in federal subsidies, receiving about $1 *billion* more than it gives (*New York Magazine*, January 23, 1995). All in all, Cobb County receives approximately $10 million dollars per day from the federal government, less than one percent of which is spent on welfare.

Out of loyalty to the notion of balance in all aspects of life, we eat and gas up before entering Cobb County, keep our visits brief, and spend as little money as possible there. With that caveat, our tour begins.

We really have only a few special things on our list here. The Big Chicken in Marietta is at the Kentucky Fried Chicken at 12 North Cobb Parkway. Downed by a storm in 1992, a vote was taken to see if the original chicken should be replaced by a more modern version. The original won. Please note that no federal or county funds paid for the restoration of the Big Chicken. The fifteen foot red chicken comb from the old Big Chicken can be seen at Central Scrap, at the intersection of Marietta and Northside in Atlanta (also the site of Atlanta's surrender in the War Between the States).

The Roswell Mill, located at the intersection of routes 20 and 9, is 20 miles north of Atlanta. The historic mill chronicles the early cotton era of pre-Civil War days. General Sherman destroyed it in 1864, but the mill was rebuilt and worked until the 1970s. Ruins of the old mill are still standing. Now Roswell Mill is filled with shops and hosts summer outdoor concerts. For information, call 642-6140.

We really like Kennesaw because it makes us nervous. All Kennesaw heads of households are required to own a gun. Kennesaw is also home to Wildman's Civil War (and KKK supply) store, the Big Shanty Museum, and "The General," locomotive of Andrew's Raiders fame. Many other historic sites dot the landscape of this important town (formerly known as Big Shanty), and it's well worth the visit.

Our final foray into the wilds of Newt's 6th Congressional District takes us to the quintessential Dixie Speedway in Woodstock. Call 926-5315 for information and directions. The speedway, featuring a dirt track and loud cars racing round and round, also offers the demolition derby, spectator racing (where drivers in their souped-up family cars race each other), and the chain race. The chain race is unique. Three cars are loosely chained together. The first has an engine and no brakes. The second, nothing. The third, just brakes. Four or five of these sets get on the track and attempt to race around it. You can imagine the possibilities! We love the Dixie Speedway on a warm summer night, but beware of the snacks! Hot dog buyers can expect their dog to come already slathered in catsup. Bleah!

Finally, we present a list of **Large Structures of Georgia:**

**Fruit n' Nuts:**

| | |
|---|---|
| Big Apple | Main Street, Cornelia. Route 123 off 441. |
| Big Peach | I-75 and route 49, south of Macon. |
| Big Peanut | I-75 and route 112, south of Andersonville. |

**Mammals:**

| | |
|---|---|
| Big Chicken | KFC, 12 North Cobb Parkway, Marietta. |
| Big Rabbitt | Route 13, Rabbittown (Gainesville). |
| Br'er Rabbitt | Routes 129/441, south of I-20, Eatonton. |
| Big Eagle | Rock Eagle 4-H Center, route 441 between Madison & Eatonton. |
| Big Guitar Players | Highway 138, north of Conyers. |
| Big Generals | Stone Mountain. |

**Big Fish:**

| | |
|---|---|
| Big Salmon | Pharr Road at Fish Market, between Peachtree and Piedmont, Atlanta. |

**Balls:**

| | |
|---|---|
| Big Golfball | I-85 at exit 11, Palmetto, just south of Atlanta. |

# Suggested Reading List

American Institute of Architects. *AIA Guide to the Architecture of Atlanta.* Athens, Georgia: University of Georgia Press, 1993.

Allen, Ivan. *Atlanta From the Ashes.* Atlanta: Ruralist Press, 1929.

American Guide Series. *Atlanta: A City of the Modern South, a WPA Guide.* New York: Smith & Durrell, 1942.

Clarke, E.Y. *Illustrated History of Atlanta.* Atlanta: Cherokee Publishing Company, 1877.

Cothran, Betty. *Destinations, Detours & Diversions.* Flowery Branch, Georgia: Seaworthy Publications, 1989.

Davis, Ren and Helen. *Atlanta's Urban Trails*, vol. I. Atlanta: Susan Hunter Publications, 1988.

Floyd, E. Randall. *Great Southern Mysteries.* Little Rock, Arkansas: August House, 1989.

Foner, Eric. *A Short History of the Reconstruction.* New York: Harper & Row, 1990.

Jenkins, James. *Murders and Social Change.* Atlanta, Paje Publications, 1974.

Galphin, Bruce. *The Riddle of Lester Maddox.* Atlanta: Camelot Publishing Company, 1968.

Garrett, Franklin M. *Atlanta and its Environs*, vols. I & II. Athens, Georgia: University of Georgia Press, 1954.

Harsh, George. *Lonesome Road.* New York: Norton & Company, 1971.

Huie, John, Jr. *The Dream of Lester Maddox.* Emory University: MA Thesis, 1970.

Jenkins, James S. *Murder in Atlanta.* Atlanta: Cherokee Publishing Company, 1981.

Kirby, Jack Temple. *Media-Made Dixie: The South in the American Imagination.* Baton Rouge, Louisiana: Louisiana State University Press, 1978.

Kuhn, Clifford M., Harlon E. Joye, and E. Bernard West. *Living Atlanta: An Oral History of the City, 1914-1948.* Athens, Georgia: University of Georgia Press, 1990.

Martin, Charles H. *The Angelo Herndon Case and Southern Justice.* Baton Rouge, Louisiana: Louisiana State University Press, 1976.

Mitchell, George. *Ponce de Leon.* Atlanta: Argonne Books, 1983.

Mixon, G.L. *The Atlanta Riot of 1906.* 2 vols. University of Cincinnati: Doctoral Dissertation, 1989.

O'Briant, Don. *Looking for Tara.* Marietta, Georgia: Longstreet Press, 1994.

Paideia School. *Patches and Squares of Ponce de Leon.* Atlanta: Paideia School, 1985.

Pyron, Darden Asbury. *Southern Daughter: The Life of Margaret Mitchell.* London: Oxford University Press, 1991.

Reagan, Alice E. *H.I. Kimball, Entrepreneur.* Atlanta, Georgia: Cherokee Publishing Company, 1983.

Sawyer, Elizabeth M. and Jane Foster Matthews. *The Old in New Atlanta.* Atlanta, Georgia: JEMS Publications, 1976.

Schwartz, Maryln. *A Southern Belle Primer.* New York: Doubleday, 1991.

Spalding, Phinizy. *Georgia: The WPA Guide to Its Towns and Countryside.* Columbia, South Carolina: University of South Carolina Press, 1990.

Strait, Raymond. *Here They Are - Jayne Mansfield.* New York: SPI Books/Shapolsky Publications, Inc., 1992.

Wilson, Charles Reagan and William Ferris. *Encyclopedia of Southern Culture.* Chapel Hill, North Carolina: University of North Carolina Press, 1989.

Woodworth, Karl and Linda. *Find Your Own Way in Downtown Atlanta.* Atlanta, Georgia: Conger Printing Company, 1976.

# Reader Participation Notice

We would welcome input from our readers for the second edition of *Sideways Atlanta*. We know we skipped a lot of great stuff and we suspect there are still many things we don't yet know about. If there is anything you feel should be included, or if you have any comments, please direct them to us at:

**Sideways Atlanta
Creative Intelligence Agency
P.O. Box 77
Edinboro, PA  16412**

or e-mail us at:
winterberger@edinboro.edu

We would love to hear from you!

**Additional copies of *Sideways Atlanta* may be ordered for $9.95 plus $2.00 shipping and handling per book. Your check or money order should be payable to the Creative Intelligence Agency.**

Work has also begun on our next project, *The Spiral Sliced South*. Similar in content and format to *Sideways Atlanta*, we again welcome advice, suggestions, and tips.

# About the Authors

Suzanne Winterberger and Bill Tomey are photographers and travel enthusiasts. They began working together on this project in 1993. Both did the research and photography; Suzanne did the writing. Bill has been a resident of Atlanta since 1980. Suzanne teaches Photography at Edinboro University of Pennsylvania. She is not pleased with her status as a Yankee but does not want to make things worse by moving to Atlanta and becoming a Damn Yankee!

Bill and Suzanne on the top of Lookout Mountain